A MATTER OF SURVIVAL

A MATTER OF
SUR-VIVAL

CANADA IN THE 21st CENTURY

DIANE FRANCIS

KEY PORTER BOOKS

Canadian Cataloguing in Publication Data

Francis, Diane, 1946-
A matter of survival: Canada in the twenty-first century

Includes index.
ISBN 1-55013-471-X

1. Economic history - 1990- . 2. Industrial productivity. 3. International economic relations. 4. Economic policy. I. Title.

HC59.15.F73 1993   330.9'049   C93-094124-1

Key Porter Books Limited
70 The Esplanade
Toronto, Ontario
Canada M5E 1R2

The publisher gratefully acknowledges the assistance of the Canada Council and the Ontario Arts Council.

Design: Annabelle Stanley
Printed and bound in Canada

93 94 95 96 97 98 6 5 4 3 2 1

CONTENTS

PREFACE

THIS BOOK IS ABOUT THE ACCELERATING AND FRIGHT-
ening changes underway in the world's economy and
how Canada is badly out of sync with the new reality. The germ for this project was contained in a letter I wrote to publisher Anna Porter in early 1992,
outlining the many reasons why I could not undertake a revised version of my book on Canadian stock market
investments. I declined to embark on this follow-up project,
I wrote in my letter, because economic shifts were happening so rapidly that such a book would never be timely and
up-to-date.

I also cited the reasons that the election of New Domocratic
Party governments in several provinces, the nagging sepa-
ratist problem, and soaring government deficits had eliminated many incentives to invest in Canadian stocks, or even
to keep all of one's capital in Canadian dollars. Because of
such concerns, smart money was being put into other currencies, or invested in mutual funds with offshore interests, or
in Canadian oil and gold-mining companies because they
were paid in U.S. dollars for their commodities.

That smart money was correct. By the end of 1992, Canada's currency had been devalued 11 per cent, from US$0.88 to US$0.78, and oil, gold, and offshore mutual funds had skyrocketed in value. More devaluations and a dramatic lowering of living standards will afflict Canadians in the 1990s unless the country dismantles both its political and its welfare-state structure. That does not mean turning the country into a sweatshop or eliminating its health benefits, but, without massive reform, Canadians face a debt crisis sometime in the 1990s. And debts increase wages, prices, and taxes, which hurts our competitiveness in the expanding global marketplace.

This book is not a definitive study of global or historical events. It is my idiosyncratic analysis of the news noise around us — why it has occurred and what it means — based on travels and interviews over the past few years. Those observations have led me to conclude that Canada is badly, and dangerously, losing ground, and that to regain our footing Canadians must understand what's going on, become more efficient, and start to hustle for markets worldwide.

CANADA NOW

CANADIANS MAY BE THE LUCKIEST PEOPLE ON EARTH, BUT
we are also among the world's most mismanaged
and spoiled. Canada has never been saddled with a
huge, lawless underclass or burdened with monstrous global military responsibilities. It has never
been destroyed by wars or invaded by millions of
refugees sneaking across its border. Until anti-investment
policies were instituted in the 1970s and early 1980s, this
country's economic growth was impressive, thanks mostly to
massive U.S. and other foreign investment. Since the War of
1812, Canada has never been victimized by an aggressive,
hostile neighbour. Living without fear of invasion, Canada
has been free to develop markets in the United States, or
anywhere else, and to go about its business peacefully.

Smug and prosperous, Canada squats atop North
America, a gigantic and cold piece of real estate occupied
by the world's most liberal "Americans." For years, Canada's
growing population, now numbering 27 million, has divided
the spoils from a vast, resource-rich hinterland that foreigners helped them to exploit. Now, as then, most

Canadians live in cities within 160 kilometres of the United States and have a symbiotic relationship with their American cousins. In essence, Canadians have benefited from U.S. economic know-how and capital while enjoying life in a European-style social-welfare state.

But proximity to the United States is both a blessing and a curse. Canada's economy has become integrated with its neighbour's. Canada is the biggest trading partner of the United States, and vice versa. But Canada, one-twelfth the size of its neighbour economically, is proportionately more dependent on the United States than the other way around. About 25 per cent of Canada's economy is generated by trade, with 80 per cent of these goods and services destined for the U.S. market. Only 8 per cent of the U.S. economy is dependent upon trade, with the entire world. The relationship is distinctly one-sided: Canada must adapt to U.S. policies, not the other way around.

As trade between the two nations increases, as it has under free trade, Canadian politicians have less discretion to adjust taxation and monetary policies than before. If Canadian politicians were allowed to spend whatever they wanted and print money as needed, the money would decrease in value. This is called inflation. Some 40 per cent of the $630 billion our governments have borrowed is owed to foreign lenders, whom we pay back in Canadian dollars. When our dollar drops in value by 11 per cent, they take a cut of 11 per cent when converting payments back into their currency. This is what lenders call a haircut. And, in 1992, Canada's foreign lenders took an 11 per cent haircut, with the result that they demanded more interest to offset the possible risk of further depreciation in the future. Interest rates Canadian governments pay are higher in 1993 than the rates U.S. governments pay. This means Canadian businessmen, homeowners, and consumers who borrow are at a disadvantage, compared with their U.S. counterparts.

The problem is that Canadian governments have run out of savings to borrow in Canada and so must turn to foreign lenders for most of what they need. And, with nearly $60 billion in additional debt added to the books in 1993 in the form of deficits ($35 billion federal, $9 billion Ontario, and the rest spread among the other provinces and the municipalities), we are in for higher and higher interest rates or a dramatically lower currency.

Government overspending in Canada is the primary reason that our interest rates and taxes are higher than those which Americans pay. It is frustrating that successive Canadian governments, both federal and provincial, have ignored, or failed to understand, the fact that changes taking place outside their borders virtually dictate what they must do at home. This ignorance has put Canada in the position of undergoing a profound correction, or lowering, of living standards, driven in large measure by massive tax avoidance on the part of its citizens. Canada's taxation and interest-rate levels are dangerously out of step with its neighbour's. Neither people nor their capital can be held captive in a jurisdiction like Canada's where taxes, as a proportion of GDP, are 10 per cent higher than those of its neighbour.

As taxes have been increased, they have yielded less as a result of tax avoidance, which has created the need for ever higher taxes, in turn causing more tax avoidance. It's a vicious circle the country cannot escape unless spending is ruthlessly cut or a Berlin Wall is erected between the two countries to "imprison" Canadian shoppers, tourists, businesses, and capital. About 40 per cent of Canada's GDP is paid in taxes compared with 30 per cent in the United States. A Canadian is someone who loves the country's health care system but buys cheaper goods in the United States whenever possible and vacations or retires in Florida. A Canadian business person who cannot compete with his or her U.S. counterparts because their taxes, land, and wage costs are lower has the option of moving to or expanding in the United States and must, to save the business. This situation is economically ruinous for the country, and happens mainly because Canadian taxes are higher than those in the United States.

The single best example of avoidance involves Canada's excessive taxation of cigarettes. A package of cigarettes costs Canadians about $5 at the time of writing, while that same pack of cigarettes costs about $2.50 in the United States. This price difference makes it worthwhile for the millions of Canadian smokers who live one hour from the border to go to the United States to buy cigarettes. Even worse, the Canadian government allows a person who has stayed overnight in the United States to bring back one carton of cigarettes, or 10 packs, duty free. Even non-smokers who go to the United States for more than a day bring back their quota of cigarettes and resell them to friends and associates for a profit.

The profits are so great that smuggling has become big business: it is estimated that one out of every three packs of cigarettes sold in Canada has been brought into the country by bootleggers. Illegal smokes are widely available in bars, convenience stores, and fast-food outlets, and from outdoor vendors. Hundreds of millions of dollars are lost, both in uncollected tax revenues and in spending to support the cost of police investigations and criminal prosecutions. This illustrates, as did prohibition in the 1920s in the United States, the folly of policies that fly in the face of market behaviour. People will smoke. Tax will be avoided. No amount of money can ensure adequate policing of the world's longest undefended border. And if there's a buck to be made smuggling, people will do it.

The discrepancy between Canadian and U.S. sales taxes is another case in point. In Canada, sales taxes average 15 per cent (the goods and services tax of 7 per cent, plus an average of 8 per cent provincial sales tax, everywhere but Alberta). By contrast, U.S. states tax at anywhere from 4 to 6 per cent, and there is no federal sales tax. Obviously, attempting to finance government expenditures through sales taxes that are significantly higher than those in the neighbouring jurisdiction is simply asking for trouble. Studies in the European Community show that, where the VAT (Value Added Tax) differs between two bordering countries by 4 per cent or more, smuggling becomes rampant. Clearly, the higher taxes go in Canada, the less revenue they generate, because smuggling and tax avoidance have become second nature to Canadians.

Since cigarette taxes were pushed through the roof and the goods and services tax was introduced, estimated annual spending of $6 billion in cross-border shopping has occurred. Snowbirds living in Florida or other sunbelt climes in winter spend an estimated $10 billion annually for U.S. goods and services, and that does not include spending by tourists drawn to the United States by cheaper prices as well as climate or various other attractions. These tax-driven behaviours outweigh the $14-billion net export income Canada collects from the United States in peak years. So, whatever Canada exports to earn its keep in the world is totally offset because our politicians don't realize that Canadians will avoid taxes whenever and however possible.

Of course, Canadian governments must levy high taxes because they spend so much. Canada has one of the world's highest debt levels, and some 40 per cent of loans to our governments are held by foreign lenders. This means that, at 7 per cent interest rates, some $17.6 billion a year will flow out of the country - more than the value of our net exports. Obviously, the Canadian economic pie is steadily shrinking. Because there is no end in sight, billions of dollars have fled the country, and an estimated 30 per cent of all money socked away in private portfolios is invested in U.S. currency bonds or stocks to hedge against future currency collapses.

Canada's political structure is more like that of a customs union than a unitary state. Ottawa functions more like the decentralized, fangless government in Brussels than like Washington, D.C. The provinces are too big and powerful. They collect more taxes than the federal government does. Canada has become, in effect, ten "countries" bound together, as in Europe, by bribes in the form of equalization payments that skim wealth from the three rich provinces for distribution to the poorer ones. This decentralization was propelled by Quebec's demand for powers equivalent to those of an independent country. The powers accorded Quebec were then given to the others.

This situation makes economic management difficult. By spending excessive amounts year after year, the Liberal and NDP regimes in Ontario from 1985 to 1993 single-handedly sabotaged efforts by the Bank of Canada and the Progressive Conservatives to control inflation, interest, and exchange rates.

Apart from wilful ignorance and a structure that makes concerted action difficult, there are other reasons why

Canada is squandering its high living standards. Few Canadian leaders have fully understood the reasons for the country's success. Canada's prosperity was a combination of luck and geography. First, Canada's distance from Europe saved its industrial base from war damage. Then, especially following the Second World War, the United States aggressively invested in our resource and manufacturing sectors.

In the 1970s, concerns about foreign investment gripped certain policy makers in Canada. Canada's Liberals embarked on nationalistic policies that discouraged foreign participation in the economy, and also created wasteful, and inefficient, public enterprises. At the same time, an unaffordable welfare state was established, resulting in huge debts and deficits, and slow economic growth.

The result is that, some time in the 1990s, a Canadian crisis of monumental proportions will occur. This is not speculation. It *will* happen, because compound interest is cannibalizing our country. By 1993, public-sector debts hit $630 billion, or 90 per cent of the GDP. At average borrowing costs of 7 per cent, debts will double by 2003, even if there are no government deficits. As a result, by the next century, Canada's debts will total $1.26 trillion, or 180 per cent more than the estimated GDP. (By contrast, it will take our $700-billion GDP 36 years to double in size.)

Obviously, the country will come unstuck. Lenders are looking elsewhere because Canada is becoming too risky and their own priorities are changing. European capital will be increasingly tied up with investing in the exciting economies of Asia and Eastern Europe. Germany, which used to buy billions of dollars' worth of Canadian bonds, is now a borrower itself, financing the exorbitant costs of unification, an unsustainable social-welfare state, and greedy unions that are driving business to Wales, Spain, North America, and Asia. Japanese and other Asian capital will be increasingly earmarked for investment in the rapidly growing economies of the East and for purchasing arms. Meanwhile, well-heeled Canadians are also investing heavily in offshore stocks and bonds or ventures as the country's currency, and prospects, deteriorate.

To bear such a burden, Canada's taxes must go higher. But this is impossible, and would cause more recession, more tax avoidance, and a flight of businesses out of the country. The only alternative is to inflate — or let deficits run so high that the dollar collapses. But eventually this latter tactic would cause a trading-partner backlash, excessive interest rates to entice foreign lenders to deal with us, more tax avoidance, business departures and, finally, a Mexican-style debt crisis. If the collapse of the dollar cannot be averted — and there are ways to do so — the results will be tragic. The flight of capital and capitalists to the United States will seriously, and perhaps permanently, injure our country. The savings of the captive middle class will be obliterated, as happened in Mexico, because Canadian currency and real-estate assets will be dramatically devalued overnight.

However, as Hungarian-born investment banker Andy Sarlos once wryly remarked to me: "The best thing about Canada is that the worst thing that can happen is that we go bust and are bailed out and become part of the United States. Every country in the world would love to have that as their only downside risk."

While sounding disloyal, Sarlos was merely being realistic. Canada is unwittingly at a crossroads. If we are to pass the baton of high living standards onto the next generation, we must realize that economic competition is ferocious. We must understand how the world evolves. We must streamline governments to save money by dismantling our provinces and welfare state. If we do not take such proactive steps, the debt crisis will force us to act anyway, and we will probably end up as Americans. Some may welcome that eventuality, but any bail-out would take place only after a great deal of pain, chaos and injury to our society and economy.

This book aims to disarm those who continue to fight the inevitable. There is no point in railing against the Americans and the globalization of the economy, or in erecting tariff barriers, opting out of trade agreements, or wishing things were like the good old days when the United States and Canada were virtually the only industrialized economies around. No one owes Canada a living. Canadians must pay their own way or become absorbed by whoever does pay it. The world is changing around us, and, as subsequent chapters will illustrate, the transformation is dramatic, immutable, and irreversible.

THE GLOBAL
ECONOMY

IN SEPTEMBER 1992, MOSCOW'S BOLSHOI CIRCUS HAD JUST finished touring Japan to wildly appreciative audience response. But, when the 12,798-ton Russian ship that was to take the circus home sailed out of Yokohama harbour, it left stranded on the dock 93 performing bears, leopards, parrots, and other animals, together with their 10 trainers. In the ship's hold, where the animals should have been, were 189 used cars, purchased by the circus's human performers for use or resale back home. The abandoned animals and their caretakers eventually found their way home on another Russian freighter.

The circus incident illustrates one of the many ways in which the world has changed in the last few years. Under the old Soviet regime, people devoted years to becoming circus performers, animal trainers, world-class athletes, and ballet dancers. These occupations enjoyed high status in the communist world, along with scientists, army officers, and

1 1

political *apparatchiks*. These people were given the opportunity to purchase a car, occupy a comfortable apartment, and take holidays in exclusive resorts on the Black Sea. After the Iron Curtain fell in 1989, such perquisites were no longer available as the people of the former communist state were plunged into a form of *laissez-faire* capitalism and left to their own devices. In the scramble to adjust to the new economic environment, circus performers were prepared to abandon their privileged roles in order to seize a valuable commodity. It was all very well to be a lion-tamer, but a Toyota was worth hard cash.

The former Soviet Union is not the only region in the world that has been thrown into disarray by the new world economy. And circus performers are not the only ones looking for new ways to make money. Businesses everywhere have been shifting gears in order to survive. So have other countries. Socialist states such as China and Vietnam have been transforming themselves into capitalist systems. India and Mexico have thrown open their doors to foreign investment for the first time in modern history. Japan and Germany, demilitarized since the end of the Second World War, have been contemplating building up their armed forces and expanding their military role. The end of the Cold War triggered a global recession as the world's economy underwent a profound and permanent restructuring.

Freer trade is long established among non-communist countries and is here to stay. It arises, in large measure, from a need for international cooperation following high-profile threats to global peace and economics posed by tyrants such as Saddam Hussein or events which preceded the Gulf War. Then there's the collapse of the Iron Curtain — the biggest postwar shock of all to the global economy — which has sparked the Yugoslavian civil war and the need for the world's countries to provide aid and trade opportunities. On the plus side, the end of the Cold War set people free from tyranny and removed the immediate threat of nuclear war. On the downside, the end of the Cold War has exposed environmental degradation, sparked a rise in nationalism, and led to political unrest. It also has caused huge migrations of people fleeing war and economic deprivation.

Even as the world was, it seemed, falling apart, there were some truly wonderful developments. Democracies were replacing dictatorships which had enslaved billions of people for decades. Perhaps most important - and easily forgotten - was the disappearance of the Soviet Union, which ended the unsustainable arms race that had threatened the survival of the planet itself.

The end of the Cold War meant that mankind was like a family that had finally paid off its mortgage: once the threat of impoverishment was removed, family members were forced to deal with other problems, both domestic and global. And how family members have been dealing with those problems preoccupies our political and business leaders as the century nears its end. They have been trying to cope with and understand the profound and irreversible economic shifts and societal earthquakes that are transforming civilization.

And so must we all.

THE WORLD'S ECONOMIC CONSTITUTION

The economic transformation of the world began in 1944 when representatives from 28 Allied nations met in the village of Bretton Woods, New Hampshire, to talk about free trade. This unprecedented meeting was made necessary because the Allies had restructured their economies in order to defeat the Nazis and Japanese. For the first time in history, food, clothing, vehicles, armaments, and other materials flowed, tariff free, from one country to another. At the same time that they were removing tariff barriers, the Allied nations reorganized their manufacturing base along global lines for security reasons and for greater efficiency. Wings for aeroplanes were made in one country, propeller blades in another, fuselages in a third, and the different parts were then assembled in a fourth. Weapons and ammunition, too, were manufactured wherever the workforce was most efficient, the raw materials were most accessible, and other natural advantages prevailed. Prior to the war, such economic cooperation among sovereign nations was non-existent. After the First World War, countries protected inefficient industries by erecting tariff barriers designed to shut out import competition. This protectionism helped bring about the Great Depression of the 1930s.

The system of free trade devised at Bretton Woods for the war effort worked so well that the Allied leaders wanted to continue to enjoy its benefits. They also realized that a return to economic isolationism would make it impossible to rebuild damaged economies or replace those that had been destroyed by the war. So the Bretton Woods participants established the framework for what now is known as the GATT process. The GATT, or General Agreement on Tariffs and Trade, has become the world's economic constitution and is constantly under revision. It established the rules of trade and has been responsible over the years for steadily, and dramatically, reducing tariffs around the world among those countries that participate. The result has been an unprecedented degree of cross-ownership and interdependence among nations — the cornerstone of the global economy.

Open economies are characterized by a high degree of foreign ownership, and lowered tariffs encourage transnational companies to locate anywhere that it makes economic sense to do so. In Canada, for instance, the auto industry was non-existent until the 1965 Autopact with the United States, which required U.S. auto makers to match the percentage of auto jobs in Canada to the percentage of cars sold in Canada. In order to facilitate this, the Autopact allowed parts and cars to flow, tariff free, across the border. So, widgets made in Ohio could be exported freely to assembly plants in Ontario, and cars assembled in Ontario could be freely exported back to California or wherever else in the United States. As things turned out, labour and power rates were cheaper in Canada than in the United States, with the result that, by 1993, a greater percentage of assembly-line and parts-making jobs ended up in Canada than in the United States. But the interdependence is enormous: Canadian-owned auto-parts companies are greatly dependent upon sales to assembly plants in Canada owned by U.S., Japanese, and Korean transnationals. In 1992, exports of auto, trucks, and vehicle parts to the United States from Canada totalled C$27.062 billion out of total exports of C$118.428 billion, or nearly $1 out of every $4 worth of exports to the United States.

Conversely, Canadian corporations have invested heavily south of the border in resources, real estate, banking, and other businesses. By 1991, Canadian corporations had directly invested C$54.639 billion in the U.S. economy, and U.S. companies had invested C$83.377 billion in Canada.

The impact of foreign ownership on Canada's relatively small economy is greater than that in the United States. Nonetheless, it illustrates the interdependence that can arise as a result of freer trade. The United Nations estimated that as much as one-third of the world's US$2.2 trillion trade in 1992 was simply intercorporate transfers among the 170,000 subsidiaries owned by the world's 35,000 transnational corporations. Oil from Exxon Corp.'s fields around the world are shipped to its gasoline stations in other countries. Auto parts from Germany are assembled in Brazil or Mexico.

Between the 1944 Bretton Woods arrangement and the 1990s, there have been seven GATT "rounds," or revised treaties, and membership has increased to 106 countries. With each new agreement, more trade barriers have fallen, and economic growth has increased. Only in the 1970s, when the oil price hikes by the oil cartel, OPEC, took the wind out of the world's economic sails, was there a setback in the steady progress toward greater prosperity and wealth creation.

But the recession of the 1970s was no repudiation of freer trade. The world economy, helped by continued GATT agreements, soon rebounded. Economies and trade grew for virtually all participants. Wealth and per-capita income increased steadily year after year. In 1940, the average tariff in industrial countries was 40 per cent. It fell to 24 per cent by 1950, 12 per cent by 1970, and 5 per cent by 1990. Negotiators working in 1992 hoped to lower tariffs to 1.5 per cent by the year 2000. Each drop in tariffs was accompanied by an increase in economic activity.

Before global free trade, the world was characterized by a handful of empires and economies in which only a tiny élite prospered, while the vast majority of humanity lived in abject poverty. Two generations after Bretton Woods, the world economy has created a sizeable "middle class" of nations. Some 2 billion people, out of a global population of 5.2 billion, live in relative comfort or outright luxury.

Of course, there are still 3.2 billion people living in desperate poverty. Many people in Africa and the Middle East are destitute, with little economic or political freedom, and little hope of reform. Only political enlightenment, trade, and aid can help them. But middle classes are growing in India, China, and Latin America. Their 2.5 billion people are starting to benefit from political and economic shifts. China is well on its way to becoming a capitalist country, its people eating better than ever before in history. Some one-quarter of India's 840 million people, for instance, live in relative comfort: 60 million are financially better off than most Americans, and another 140 million are as wealthy as the Taiwanese or Koreans.

But GDP yardsticks can be totally misleading. Families can live on US$40 a month in Vladivostok, but not in Zurich. Just because a glass of wine in Switzerland costs US$10.00 and US$0.10 in Russia does not mean the Swiss are a hundred times richer than the Russians. They probably are, but the example points out the misleading nature of GDP figures, which are merely the sum total of goods and services in a local currency converted into its market value in U.S. dollars. The point is that market values do not reflect purchasing power. In 1993, the International Monetary Fund measured economies in purchasing-price equivalencies and came up with some surprising results. Based on this measure, China, for instance, has an economy bigger than Germany's and only slightly smaller than Japan's, and Mexico's is significantly larger than Canada's. The point is that GDP and other macroeconomic measurements don't tell the whole tale. The world is better off than ever before in history, despite its huge population, thanks primarily to trade.

But something strange is emerging. Even as freer trade through GATT draws nations closer together economically, the world appears to be dividing itself into three regional trading blocs — East Asia, North America, and Europe — called the "Triad." Seemingly at odds with free trade, the Triad actually arises out of the GATT; these blocs form among countries who wish to speed up the GATT process by lowering tariffs among themselves more quickly. Leading this trend is the European Community, whose 12 members eliminated tariff barriers on January 1, 1993. Customs inspections of goods moving within Europe is no longer required. But goods flowing into the European Community from North America or Japan, or elsewhere, will be subject to duties, tariffs, taxes, and inspection, according to GATT rules.

Similar trading blocs are being discussed by countries in Asia. In North America, the Canada–U.S. trade deal and the proposed North American Free Trade Agreement (NAFTA) with Mexico, if passed, will eventually eliminate tariffs on most goods traded. Unlike the European Community, however, North Americans have pulled their punches and have excluded from free, unfettered trade such sectors as beer, culture, and certain agricultural products. Eventually, the goal will be the same as that in Europe — free flow within North America, but duties, tariffs, taxes, and inspection, according to GATT rules, on goods from elsewhere.

While the Triad is a logical extension of the GATT process, it is also protectionist by default. That is because outsiders face a tariff on their goods, whereas companies located inside the trading bloc do not. The decided advantage that Triad residents enjoy has resulted in tensions and resentments, but has also caused other regions to look at similar set-ups or to locate facilities inside blocs. This trend will continue unless GATT moves quickly toward free trade worldwide. And, in 1993, that looked increasingly unlikely as the global recession spread to new countries.

GLOBAL SHOCKS

The world became smaller in 1974 when a mushroom cloud formed over a remote region of India. The Canadian government had sold India two experimental nuclear reactors in good faith. But the Indian government, frightened of its communist and Moslem neighbours, used this technology to make its own nuclear bomb. The Western world recoiled at the thought that a third-world nation in a volatile region could possess a weapon of mass destruction. Canada refused to complete the reactors or to supply India with uranium until the country signed the Nuclear Non-proliferation Treaty. India refused to sign.

This was one of five "shocks" between 1968 and 1975 which demanded international cooperation and profoundly changed the global economy, according to University of Toronto professor John Kirton: "There was the oil shock; the removal of gold bullion as backing for the U.S. dollar; America's abandonment of its South Vietnamese allies in 1975; its earlier and humiliating defeat in the 1968 Tet offensive against tiny North Vietnam; and the explosion of a nuclear device in India."

The most significant of the shocks to which Professor

Kirton refers was the humiliation of the United States in the Vietnam War, because it undermined belief and confidence in America's postwar power and hegemony. As a result, a shift occurred in the balance of both political and economy power in the world, and America's postwar adolescent attitude that it was invincible and chosen to right the world's wrongs was dramatically eroded.

The atrocities committed by the Americans and their South Vietnamese allies were beamed nightly during the eight years of war into U.S. living rooms. National celebrities joined young, educated Americans in protesting against the war. Authorities often reacted violently to these demonstrations, most visibly when police beat up protesters at the Democratic Party's national convention in Chicago in 1968, and when the National Guard murdered four protesters at Kent State University in Ohio in 1970. When, finally, an ex-Marine, William Calley, blew the whistle about the My Lai massacre of innocent Vietnamese women and children by U.S. soldiers, the nation turned against an ugly war. It simply no longer believed the official argument that the war was needed for the benefit of the Vietnamese people. That revelation, combined with the large-scale protests, embarrassed Washington, destroyed the presidency of Lyndon Johnson, and humiliated the U.S. military.

The withdrawal in defeat from Vietnam in 1973 led to more U.S. humiliations and economic costs. The war was responsible in large measure for causing the other shocks. The abandonment by the United States of the gold standard was undertaken to allow Washington to inflate its currency to help pay for the Vietnam war without raising taxes. It led, in turn, to increased volatility in international financial markets. Following the Vietnam débâcle, tin-pot dictators in countries around the world — for example, in Chile, Indonesia, and, most importantly, the Persian Gulf — tested U.S. resolve by nationalizing or confiscating scores of U.S.-owned plants and assets. The United States appeared to be powerless to protect its interests. Most significantly, as the war wound down and appeared unwinnable, Arab and other oil-producing nations began to demand control and ownership of their oil fields. Not coincidentally, in 1972 the cartel launched a series of price hikes that held the U.S. and the global economy to ransom over the course of the decade. Soaring energy costs created stagflation — a deadly combination of stagnant economic growth and inflation. As well, a massive redistribution of wealth from industrialized nations to oil-producing ones took place; much of that wealth was squandered by their corrupt leaders on arms purchases and luxuries for themselves. Arguably, the failure of the United States to defend South Vietnam from the communist hordes fanned further fears among many countries, such as India, that Russian or Chinese communists could invade them with impunity. This concern undoubtedly led to India's constructing of the nuclear bomb as a means of defence.

These and other cataclysmic developments convinced the five biggest industrialized countries — the United States, France, Britain, Japan, and Germany — to join forces. France inaugurated the first economic summit in 1976, forerunner of the G-7, which includes Italy and Canada. By 1993, 18 summits had been held. These meetings constitute, in effect, baby steps toward a global government.

The G-7 functions like the world's cabinet. Although it has no legislature or stand-alone bureaucracy, and is subject to legislative scrutiny from elsewhere, decisions reached behind closed doors affect the world profoundly. For

instance, U.S. president George Bush called his G-7 counterparts after Saddam Hussein invaded Kuwait in August
1990 and obtained pledges of support, manpower, or money
from all six of them. Armed with that commitment, Bush
then had the military initiative to push Hussein back into
Iraq rubberstamped by the United Nations to gain more
help. While the G-7's support for the war didn't force U.N.
members to vote in its favour, it certainly showed that the
most powerful leaders were discussing international matters among themselves first, making up their minds, and pre-
senting the case to the rest of the world.

THE REVOLUTION OF 1989

The single most stunning series of events since the Second
World War has been the dismantling of the Soviet empire.
Television viewers around the world watched in amazement
and confusion in the fall of 1989 as, one after another, the
former Eastern-bloc countries shed communism. It was
amazing because it happened without much violence. People
took to the streets, then took over the government, without
having to face Soviet tanks and soldiers as they had in
Hungary in 1956 and Czechoslovakia in 1968.

The peaceful outcome of these uprisings was all the more
surprising in light of events on June 3 and 4, 1989, when an
estimated 5,000 students and workers in Beijing's Tiananmen
Square were massacred in a violent crackdown by China's
army. The violence came two weeks after the Chinese government had declared martial law and warned crowds to
call off their protests. Battle-hardened troops were imported
from other regions, and around midnight, civilians were

attacked by army tanks. Hundreds of pro-democracy activists were arrested in the weeks that followed.

Moscow, however, refused to interfere militarily to prop up its puppet regimes, and each was replaced with a government led by a democratically minded leader. Least surprising, perhaps, was the fact that the Soviet Union itself began to disintegrate. On March 11, 1990, Lithuania's parliament declared unilateral independence. An August 1991 coup temporarily stopped the liberalization process within the Soviet Union, but on January 1, 1992, the Union of Soviet Socialist Republics ended, not with a bang but a whimper.

How this all came about perplexes most people. Gunther Von Lojewski, chairman of Germany's public television network, maintains that historians will call this the "video revolution." Von Lojewski suggested in May 1990 that the collapse of communism was caused in large part by the video camera.

"All revolutions begin in a radio or television station," he said. "The video camera simply speeded this one up. The electronic mass media played a more major role than historians realize. I will give you a simple example. We gave for years — for no money — some 9,900 news items a year to the Eastern-bloc radio and television stations. They would change the voice-over and say, for instance, that student unrest in Berkeley was a protest against capitalism, which was not true. But the people could see for themselves the fact that police were letting a demonstration occur and that people could think for themselves. They would also see miniskirts, cars, or buildings which were more beautiful than anything in their countries. It made them realize that the propaganda they heard, to the effect that the capitalist system was so bad, couldn't be true. The camera made them realize that what they were told didn't match what their eyes could see."

In Toronto, in early 1990, shortly after the Berlin Wall came down, the British actor Peter Ustinov told a charming story which illustrates how communist leaders, too, became disillusioned. Ustinov, the son of Russian émigrés who fled Lenin's Revolution, related what his friend the late British novelist Graham Greene had prophesied. Greene noted that the Soviet Union's brightest and most ambitious individuals joined the KGB or became Communist Party leaders and travelled. "Greene said to me in the early 1980s that 'the Iron Curtain would fall in our lifetimes,' and my eyebrows hit my hairline," joked Ustinov. "But he explained it this way: 'Their best minds are in the KGB and government and they have been living all over the world to watch us. And one cannot watch without noticing.' He turned out to be quite right."

Back in 1983, Mikhail Gorbachev, then Soviet agriculture minister, was one of the Communist Party leaders who "noticed" during a memorable trip to Canada. "Perestroika was born in Canada," said Russian journalist and author Artyom Borovic in an interview in Moscow in early 1992. "Gorbachev came to Canada to visit with his close friend who was ambassador . . . there and the two talked about what changes were needed in their country. Canada was a model country."

The abject withdrawal in 1989 of Soviet troops from Afghanistan, comparable in some ways to the departure of U.S. troops from Vietnam, also prepared the way for the dissolution of the Soviet Empire. It demonstrated graphically that Soviet military might was useless against a ragtag scattering of guerrilla warriors in a third-world setting. Moscow had secretly invaded the country years before and, as was its custom, intended to keep the truth about its action from the Soviet public through its finely honed propaganda machine. But U.S. president Jimmy Carter utilized the most high-profile event in the world - the Olympic Games - to protest the Afghanistan invasion. Carter imposed a controversial boycott of the 1980 Olympics, sabotaging the event, which had never before been staged in Moscow. It was a brilliant manoeuvre. Millions of Soviet citizens, watching the games, could hardly not notice that U.S. athletes, long their chief rivals for Olympic glory, were conspicuously absent. And they were bound to wonder why.

"The significance of the Afghanistan war is that Moscow for the first time was caught lying to the people," Artyom Borovic said. In his book about the invasion of Afghanistan, *The Hidden War*, Borovic maintained that the Soviet élites were completely demoralized by the conflict.

"The public was upset too, because for years thousands of young soldiers were going to the Afghanistan front and the government was telling them that the soldiers were there helping the Afghanis build schools and hospitals. But the soldiers were coming back without limbs, with stories of atrocities, or were not coming back at all."

Moscow's defeat in Afghanistan exposed its vulnerability. Months after the withdrawal, Hungary tested Russian resolve by allowing East German tourists to leave for the West without visas. Uncontested, this trickle turned into a flood, and East Germans began pouring into Hungary, and out again to freedom. The Russians did nothing, and East Germans began to stream across their own border into West Germany too. Soon East Germans hit the streets with huge protests, involving hundreds of thousands of people, demanding freedoms. Gorbachev announced that Eastern-bloc regimes would not be defended by military force. By November 1989, the Hungarians, East Germans, Czechs, Poles, Rumanians, Bulgarians, and Yugoslavs had, mostly without violence, overthrown their communist oppressors.

THE NEW WORLD ORDER

Exhilaration shone on the faces of the Eastern Europeans who demonstrated, or fought, for reforms during those dramatic events in 1989. The Berlin Wall was torn down. Soviet flags were destroyed, and national flags unfurled. Busts of Lenin and Marx were toppled. In Rumania, cheering crowds in the grimy streets welcomed the news that brutal dictator Nicolae Ceausescu and his wife had been executed. But, in one telling news clip, Polish steelworkers gleefully took their welding torches to a plaque which dedicated their steel mill to the communist cause. Three years later, they were all thrown out of work, their mill closed for lack of business from Russia. The steelworkers, jubilant at the Cold War's end, were among its first casualties.

Up to 30 per cent of the Eastern-bloc's economy was tied to production for the Soviet Union. Most of that production was for military purposes. Typical was the Czech aeroplane enterprise Morovan Inc., whose president explained their predicament in an interview in August 1992. "We have no customers, but we have good craftsmen, and make very good airplanes," he said. "We just need help. Anyone's help."

Morovan had been part of the Bata empire before the Second World War, and in August 1992 its officials invited family head Tom Bata Sr. to a demonstration of their aerobatic and crop-duster aircraft. Bata had escaped from Czechoslovakia in 1938, just hours before the Nazis occupied the country, and moved the family's shoe-making businesses to Canada. Now Bata Inc. is a global conglomerate, with 67,000 workers in 60 countries. Morovan officials hoped they could convince their rich and well-connected fellow Czech, Bata, to buy their factory or to find someone else who would.

Hundreds of employees attending the airshow watched Bata as if he were a rock star. They gathered along the tarmac, eager to shake his hand and chat with him, and some hoisted their children on their shoulders to make sure they got a glimpse of him. The company's 1,500 workers had little else to do these days. There had been layoffs, and the remaining workforce was reduced to a four-day work week. The hangars were empty.

Uncomfortably cast in the role of a monied messiah, Bata spent the entire morning talking with company officials about the planes and production facilities. He had already told them that he had no interest in Morovan. He was sufficiently occupied as chairman of a multinational shoe manufacturing and retail empire. "I have no idea whether this factory has life," he reported later. "But I certainly will make a special effort to help them find a buyer, partner, or markets. For emotional reasons," he said.

There is no doubt that the Cold War had brought prosperity to some sectors of the global economy both within the communist bloc and outside it. With the breakdown of the Soviet Empire, Morovan lost the chief customer for its aeroplanes. Several thousand kilometres away, a comparable phenomenon was taking place. Since 1989, the State of

California has lost a net 700,000 manufacturing jobs, mostly as a result of the depression in its defence industry. California real estate values have collapsed. The state's deficit soared to a record $12.32 billion, owing to the costs of welfare and health care for the unemployed, and California legislators fought for months over spending cuts.

From 1946 to 1989, the ideological battle between the United States and Union of Soviet Socialist Republics employed millions of people, both directly and indirectly. Billions of dollars and rubles were spent on weapons and materiel and billions more on aid handed out by the two superpowers to buy allegiance from strategically important third-world countries. Trillions of dollars were squandered waging wars or financing underground guerrilla actions to fight for, or fend off, communism in Vietnam, Afghanistan, Latin America, Asia, Africa, and the Middle East. While despicable, fighting the ideological war provided a handsome living for many people.

Not only did the war machines seize up when the Cold War ended, but third-world countries also lost Cold War aid, trade privileges, and favours. They now had to shift political gears. India, a socialist country with strong trade and aid ties with the Soviet Union, opted in 1992 for market reform and opened up its economy to foreign investment. South Africa, tolerated by the United States for its anti-communist activity in southern Africa, suddenly was unable to claim U.S. support after Marxist regimes folded in neighbouring countries. Its white-controlled government sought, and obtained, a mandate in 1992 to negotiate power sharing with the black majority.

The Cold War's ruins also left penniless Soviet comrades such as Cuba, Nicaragua, Ethiopia, Angola, China, Eastern

Europe, and the 14 republics outside Russia. Now they must fend for themselves. Having lost Soviet markets and foreign aid, they defaulted on their debts to the world's bankers, which put upward pressure on interest rates worldwide. Worse yet, these countries must be lent money to buy Western goods and services. The former communist regimes in Eastern Europe have been plunged into a depression: since 1990, their economies have shrunk in size 30 per cent or more, which helped to drag the developed world into recession.

Yet another harmful consequence of the Cold War's end has been the dumping of commodities onto the world market by the Russians and their former compatriots in order to earn hard currency. This has depressed the prices of many items, from nickel to aluminium to oil, creating economic harm all over the world. Inco Limited, Canada's nickel giant, has been one of the companies hardest hit by the practice. Inco limped through most of 1992 and 1993, hobbled by calamitous price drops resulting from Russian nickel dumping. Inco faced a double whammy as aid-starved Cuba proceeded with plans to cut down its sugarcane fields and exploit its vast nickel ore body to make up for the loss of Russian subsidies. Similarly, Alcan suffered losses after the Russians began to dump aluminium.

The ending of the Cold War has had more than economic consequences. The end of the Soviet dominion sparked the continuing tragedy in the Balkans. Ethnic fighting among the former Yugoslav states has resulted in the death of tens of thousands of people, and the dislocation of two million. The peacekeeping and relief efforts cost the international community, acting through the United Nations, $1 billion a year. Similar ethnic conflicts have erupted in the former

Soviet republics of Georgia and Armenia.

Even before the Soviet Union disappeared, Iraq's Saddam Hussein had tested the new world order by invading Kuwait in August 1990. Hussein calculated that the removal of the Soviet threat diminished the U.S. interest in the Middle East, but that proved to be a miscalculation. The United States, and Europe, were more interested than ever. Both face the prospect of declining reserves of cheap oil. The spectre of a tyrant like Hussein controlling the world's oil-export price and holding the world to ransom again was intolerable. Within days of the Iraqi invasion, the United States and other G-7 members pledged manpower or money to the cause, and within weeks the United Nations rubberstamped the Gulf War initiative. Despite its brevity, the Gulf War in early 1991 cost a total of $73.2 billion, stealing capital from an already-reeling world economy.

The new "world order" is, in many ways, a world in disorder. New political boundaries are erected or erased along ethnic lines. Seemingly paradoxically, tribalism is a logical result of internationalization. Ethnic or religious groups can go it alone, or think they can, because they can plug into the global economy rather than put up with belonging to a slightly larger economy shared with other ethnic or religious groups. Boundaries are also changing because they didn't make much sense in the first place, and were arbitrary lines drawn as a result of military conquests or tyranny. A shake-out will continue, sometimes peacefully, as in the break-up of Czechoslovakia or the Soviet Union, sometimes violently, as in the break-up of Yugoslavia or in certain former Soviet republics. At the same time, political cooperation continues, as is the case in Western Europe and, to a lesser extent, in North America, as trading blocs form. The world is becoming at once more local and more global, more xenophobic and more internationalist, more cooperative and less so.

THE CHALLENGE

Cancer rates in 1990 were 10 times the Czech average in Teplice, a small city located on the Czech and East German border. Dangerous air-pollution levels kept children home from school about 40 days a year. At least once a year, students had to be evacuated to nearby villages. Several kilometres from Teplice, a village was evacuated after a chemical spill in the 1970s and the population relocated to a clump of highrises near Teplice. Central Europe's biggest petrochemical complex, built at the terminus of the Soviet oil pipeline, was located just outside Teplice. Nearby, there was a monstrous electricity-generating plant built by the Nazis and fuelled by coal mined from an adjacent, open–pit mine the size of Monaco. In the hills surrounding the pit operation, spontaneous, unattended fires burned in dumps, fuelled by dangerous, untreated chemicals. When the wind picked up, the fly ash from the mine became airborne and was so thick that I couldn't see the ornament on the hood of the taxicab in which I was a passenger. My translator, an asthmatic, coughed fitfully.

The cost of cleaning up Teplice was not the only gigantic expense facing the fledgling Republic of Czechoslovakia. Replacing its power and petrochemical sources was a staggering task. Fortunately, the complex in Teplice was on the border of wealthy Germany, concerned about excessive cancer rates in its nearby, and newly acquired, villages in former East Germany. It was hoped that Germany would one day help pay for the cost of cleaning up, or replacing, Teplice's power and petrochemical works.

But Teplice was a minor concern compared with the 70 or so nuclear reactors in Central and Eastern Europe that are considered by many observers to be totally unsafe. These could, and possibly already are, causing damage in countries hundreds or even thousands of kilometres away. Western Europeans dread another incident like that which occurred in Chernobyl, in Ukraine, where a nuclear accident killed and injured thousands of people. The fallout of radiation from Chernobyl was so high in Sweden that parents were warned against allowing their children to play out of doors for a year after the incident.

The frightening environmental problems in the former Soviet Union and Eastern-bloc countries illustrate how the actions of one country profoundly affect the environmental, as well as the economic, wellbeing of others.

Environmental damage in other parts of the world is no less severe. The Sahara desert has been spreading by up to 100 kilometres per year. Tropical deforestation totals 11.4 million hectares annually. Overpopulation has denuded entire countries of their forests. Ethiopia's forest cover declined to 1 per cent from 30 per cent, and India's from 50 per cent to 14 per cent in a century. Indications are that the world's first socioenvironmental catastrophe looms, as Africa is devoured by deserts and drought. The effect on the planet's ecosystem and climate of these and many other developments will be dire for all. The worst can be averted only through international cooperation. Such environmental problems worsen as the burgeoning human population makes demands on the earth's unsustainable resources.

In 1990, the world's population was 5.2 billion; by 2000,

it has been forecasted, it will reach 6.2 billion. At that rate of growth, the world must create 40 million jobs per year or condemn millions to starvation or unemployment in over-crowded shanty towns that threaten the environment as well as the social structure of their respective countries. Besides that, teeming populations in poor countries continue to immigrate, legally or otherwise, and crowd into the economies of wealthy neighbouring countries. This problem has contributed to fears that, in part, have led to the formation of the three regional trading blocs of the Triad: Western Europeans fear migration will soar from Central and Eastern Europe; the United States fears more boat people and illegal aliens from Mexico, the rest of Latin America, and Caribbean nations such as Haiti; and Japan, Hong Kong, Singapore, and Taiwan fear economic ruina-tion as a result of a flood of humanity should China ever become politically destabilized. Such driving forces push freer trade forward: the thinking is that, if poor neighbours are given an opportunity to sell their products to rich nations, poor people need not export themselves physically.

Although the movement toward regional freer-trade zones is unmistakable, it is a complicated process, and one that is by no means free of pain. Freer trade means the continuing movement of manufacturing activity out of rich countries and concern as to how to bootstrap — through education and retraining — the underclasses within rich countries.

The world's wealthiest economies and regions are also being invaded by uninvited immigrants, or asylum seekers. Tens of millions move annually into countries where they believe their prospects may be improved. The United States spends billions annually deploying guards along its south-ern border in a vain attempt to keep illegal aliens from

Mexico or Central and South America from entering its sputtering economy. Likewise, troops guard some Western European countries against a flood of migrants from Eastern Europe. The flow of people is driven by economic necessity or economic opportunism as the world's wretched are unwilling to wait for reforms at home or more trade openness among rich nations. These migrations are costly to rich countries because new entrants take jobs away from residents or, failing that, end up being supported as political refugees at great expense.

An equally profound adjustment is the gradual withdrawal by the United States from its postwar role of moral leader and protector. That power vacuum has led to realignments, wars, and tensions, forcing a more important role onto the United Nations and middle nations like Canada, who must provide peacekeepers and money. The U.S. desire to spend its "peace dividend" by downsizing its military presence in the world has also propelled Europe toward attempts at greater political and economic integration. No longer a potential battlefield defended by the United States, Europe must solve the problems in Central and Eastern Europe. As if to underscore U.S. insistence on Europe's independence in this regard, not one of the 150,000 U.S. troops stationed in Germany has been deployed to help control the Yugoslav conflicts, even though they are taking place only a few hundred kilometres away. Unfortunately, Europe still rarely speaks with one voice in terms of foreign policy and lacks a common armed force to implement its wishes or defend its borders.

Meanwhile, in Asia, Japan is madly investing in the region to create new markets and also to compensate for its diminished workforce, shrinking as a result of declining birthrates and lack of immigration. The Americans closed a base in the Philippines and sent jitters throughout the region. For the time being, the United States remains committed in both Japan and South Korea, partly because most costs are paid by those two countries. Unfortunately, no country in Asia can assume the role of moral and military leader. Japan is the obvious choice because of its extreme wealth, but there is resistance within Japan as well as outside the country. The facts are that Chinese, Koreans, and most others still resent and fear Japan.

As the Triad consolidates — led by the United States, Germany, and Japan — the rest of the world consists of decrepit outcasts. Africa is the only continent that saw out the 1980s worse off economically than it had been at the beginning of the decade. The growth of Islamic fundamentalism is widely feared, and should be. Latin America's people are turning to democracy and market reforms, but most nations are not out of the woods yet, with the exception of Mexico and Chile. The dozens of new Central and Eastern European countries now vying for a place in the sun are floundering and may lapse into tyranny or chaos.

Nonetheless, the world has become safer in the last few years. Now, with freer trade, it can become better too. But this will happen only if rich countries agree to a system of trade and aid which provides opportunities and facilitates wealth redistribution to the world's neediest. Without such enlightened policies, the world will continue to deteriorate into warring factions, economic outcasts, and Saddam Husseins. Like a country with a huge gap between haves and have-nots, the entire planet could become a powderkeg of rich and poor neighbourhoods, seething ghettos, bastions of safety and patches of defended turf, with too many people putting too much pressure on too few resources.

THE
TRIAD

THE AMERICAS

THE PASSAGE OF THE NORTH AMERICAN FREE TRADE Agreement (NAFTA), or some version of it, to include Mexico as well as Canada, will mark an important turning-point for the United States in its dealings with Latin America. Washington has been an insensitive bully for decades, using gunboat diplomacy and its rogue elephant, the CIA, to undermine the region's popular democratic movements. Instead of encouraging democracy, Washington supported dreadful dictators and corporate puppets who brought decades of suffering to America's other citizens.

In a sense, South and Central Americans were also casualties of the Cold War. Washington was so preoccupied with fighting communism that even the most corrupt, brutal, or undemocratic leader merely had to bill himself as an anti-communist in order to extort money from Washington in the form of secret military aid, CIA help, or Alliance for Progress programs. Commie-bashing was placed before human, or democratic, rights. The result was a foreign-policy, and human, disaster.

The Americans fostered little else. Most of Latin America went bankrupt as a result of U.S.–backed leaders who were often incompetent. Washington's paranoia about Cuba — a nation run by corrupt leaders and U.S. gangsters before communism — brought the world to the brink of World War III during the Kennedy–Khrushchev missile showdown in 1962. There was speculation that Kennedy's lukewarm interest in recapturing Cuba led to his assassination by the CIA.

Another inconsequential Latin American country — Nicaragua, with its left-leaning populist regime — caused a furore when Congress discovered that White House conspirators secretly supported a guerrilla movement to overthrow Nicaragua's government by selling arms to Iran, in contravention of congressional policy. Former president Ronald Reagan's henchmen took the blame, and were all but exonerated. The president played dumb.

But Latin America began to transform itself in the early 1980s after a series of debt crises. Military and other dictators were removed from power. International bankers began to dictate fiscal and monetary policies to the new regimes, and slowly, democracy and market reforms began to take root in some countries. Brazil's president was impeached without violence or a *coup d'état* in 1992, following press reports about his thievery. Chile's military dictator turned the country's economy around, then held free elections as promised. Argentina began to get its act together through fiscal and political reforms. Others have been equally progressive in economic terms.

But Mexico has undertaken the most dramatic about-face, abandoning its isolationism in the 1980s by joining GATT for the first time and by initiating free-trade talks with the

United States and Canada. Others in South America —
notably Brazil, Argentina, Chile, and Paraguay — have free-
trade deals and hope to join the North American arrangement.

CONTINENTAL FREE TRADE

North America's *"ménage à trois"* between Mexico, Canada,
and the United States is more of a shotgun marriage than a
match made in heaven. Canadian ambivalence toward its
increasing integration with the United States is more than
shared by Mexicans. "We are not ambivalent," comments a
Mexican entrepreneur. "We hate the Americans."

Some of this relates to old wounds. Mexico lost half its
country to the United States in the nineteenth century.
Canada was only briefly invaded during the War of 1812,
then left alone. But the identities of both Canadians and
Mexicans have been defined, in part, by anti-Americanism,
or simply the desire to not be Americans. Both Canada and
Mexico have used public enterprises and public policies to try
to avoid becoming virtual U.S. economic colonies — with
mixed results.

Then, in the 1980s, leaders in Canada, then Mexico,
decided to court the "gringos" by fully opening up their
economies to U.S. goods and services, and even ownership.
Free-trade negotiations were initiated by Brian Mulroney in
1985, and then by Mexico's president Carlos Salinas de
Gortari in 1988.

Americans were receptive to both initiatives, for economic
as well as foreign-policy reasons. Mexico and Canada can
meet the oil and other resource requirements of the United

States while providing secure markets for U.S. goods and services. An added bonus would be peace and stability along its borders. For Canada and Mexico, the deals are somewhat painful - involving greater competition for their least-efficient, tariff-protected businesses — but would also secure access to the world's biggest, and best, marketplace. Canada's trade deal merely extended access because autos and resources were already freely traded without tariffs.

Like any old married couple, the United States and Canada have had plenty of spats, but it's a match in terms of culture, language, and traditions. Mexico, in contrast, knew it would face two sceptical suitors. Canada and the United States share the world's longest undefended border. On its southern border, the United States has been building a "Berlin Wall" to keep out illegal aliens and illicit drugs from Mexico.

To become attractive to the Americans, Mexico's President Salinas, and his predecessor-mentor, former president Miguel de la Madrid, began a dramatic beautification process for Mexico, not only instituting environmental protections, but also joining GATT for the first time and waiving the usual transition period by immediately dropping tariff barriers from an average of 45 per cent to 9 per cent. Imports from the United States soared by 1992, making Mexico its third-largest trading partner, after Canada and Japan, in just a handful of years. An estimated 600,000 U.S. jobs now depend on this bilateral trade, which jumped from US$21 billion in 1987 to US$62 billion by 1992. Mexico exported US$29 billion and imported US$33.3 billion.

At the same time as it threw its doors open, Mexico mopped up its debt mess, and, in 1988, newly elected President Salinas began a series of policy changes as pervasive and painful as reforms undertaken in Poland or East

Germany. Foreign-ownership restrictions were removed, and some 800 government companies were privatized, raising US$21 billion, which was used to pay down government debts. The result is that public-sector debt has been reduced to 21 per cent of GDP with accompanying relief in burdensome interest payments. (By contrast, Canada's public-sector debts in 1993 were 92 per cent of GDP, and those of the United States, 50 per cent.) Now to keep the investment money flowing in, Mexico's government has become one of the only four governments around the world to run a budget surplus, not a deficit. Inflation went from 157 per cent in 1987 to 7 per cent by 1993, and an estimated 4 per cent in 1994, through "el pacto" — a form of wage control — which has cost Mexican workers buying power.

"We initiated the NAFTA negotiations the day we signed and concluded the first debt renegotiation in the world, among 500 commercial banks," said Salinas in an interview in May 1993. "Mexicans for generations tried to live as far as they could from the U.S. But reality proved the reverse. Millions of Mexicans had to migrate to the U.S. looking for jobs that they couldn't find in Mexico."

The courtship has been long and hard. A recession and the 1992 presidential election in the United States delayed passage, resulting in the proposed trade deal becoming a contentious political issue. And no one can guess what the U.S. Congress will do or what restraints the sidebar agreements on environment, labour standards, and import surges will contain. But NAFTA or no NAFTA, North America has been moving closer together trade-wise as Mexico deals with the pains of change.

But the microeconomic situation is another matter.

"Some 40 million Mexicans live in poverty, 17 million in

misery, and the richest one-fifth have incomes 20 times greater than the poorest one-fifth," says Patricia Nelson, respected editor of the *Mexico City News*, the country's only English-language daily newspaper. "Over 11.5 years, wages and benefits for workers have dropped 26.2 per cent in real terms from 1980."

Mexico's problem is that one million people enter the workforce every year and only 200,000 jobs are being created. Such cheap and plentiful unskilled labour will help North America regain the jobs lost to the Far East and other low-cost countries, says Salinas. But U.S. and Canadian labour spokesmen, and Ross Perot, talk of the "great sucking noise" of jobs moving north to south.

But without economic integration through free trade, America faces "the giant sucking sound" of millions of Mexicans illegally migrating forever as its economy is unable to create more jobs. For years, Americans have spent billions guarding the 3,200-kilometre border to no avail. Already an estimated one out of every five Mexicans lives, legally or otherwise, in the United States and the only way to stem the human flow is to help Mexicans create opportunities at home. And Mexicans will get, under free trade, the low-paying jobs that are now in Asia, or about to shift there. But distances are great, and Canadians and Americans suffer from huge trade deficits with the Asians. Mexicans, by contrast, are making American, and some Canadian, exporters richer.

"NAFTA is the possibility for the North American region to recover jobs that it has lost to other regions in the world that are more competitive," said Salinas, who has a doctorate in economics from Harvard University. "NAFTA is a way [to sustain] the viability [of North America] in the middle and long run. Mexicans for generations tried to live as far as they could from the U.S. Reality proved the reverse. Millions of Mexicans had to migrate to the U.S. looking for jobs that they couldn't find in Mexico. If NAFTA failed, the message for Latin America would be a very bad one."

On top of that, rejection could mean a relapse to Mexico's undemocratic policies and an unravelling of Salinas's democratic, environmental, and legal reforms. Unfortunately for Mexico, its policies have already accrued huge benefits to the United States, providing less incentive to integrate the two economies. Texas is the biggest backer of NAFTA and has created more jobs than any six states put together during the 1989–1992 recession, thanks to the newfound trade boom with Mexico. And the U.S. merchandise-trade surplus increases daily. Canada's trade relationship has also jumped, masked in part by the fact that goods exported to the United States for re-export to Mexico are not counted. Estimates are that Canada's trade with Mexico is not $750 million, but double that because of such re-exportation. The same applies to Mexican exports to Canada, bringing the trading relationship to nearly $5 billion both ways.

Fears of massive job losses with a Mexican trade deal are groundless. Tariffs at 9 per cent, on average, are useless against Mexico's lower wage rates. Already some 73 per cent of imports from Mexico to Canada enter tariff free, and the average duty is only 2.7 per cent. Besides, the Canadian Manufacturers Association says direct labour represents only 18 per cent of costs for the average manufacturer, a clear indicator that labour-intensive jobs left Canada and the United States long ago.

The cost of capital here is also exorbitant (prime rate is 55.5 per cent). Often infrastructure — ranging from telephone to postal services and garbage collection — must be replaced or circumvented at considerable cost. Likewise, corruption — whether it's the bribes sometimes requested by crooked policemen or those extorted by fire/building inspectors — adds to the cost of doing business.

Besides, labour is not as cheap — in real terms — as many believe.

"Whoever establishes in Mexico only because of the hand labour advantage is wrong," says prominent businessman Carlos Eduardo Represas, chairman of the Mexican subsidiary of Swiss giant Nestlé. "With government-required fringe benefits, wages are more than doubled and, if adjusted for productivity, unit labour costs in Mexico are only 34 per cent cheaper than [in] the U.S. in manufacturing. Canada is still the higher-cost producer in North America.

"That's only for labour, and whatever the labour-cost advantage is today won't last. Wages will go up faster here than in the U.S. and Canada because the comparative advantage of Mexico will bring jobs here," said Represas. "By 2000, we estimate Mexico's economy will be the same size as Canada's and there will be a population of 100 million earning 30 per cent more per capita."

By fall 1992, Salinastroika had attracted tens of billions in direct foreign investment, with two-thirds earmarked for manufacturing and 20 per cent for tourism projects. After the Americans, the British and German multinationals are coming in droves to hunt for opportunities through acquisitions, joint ventures, or exports.

Canada, with too few international players, has lagged somewhat, but thousands of medium-sized enterprises and individuals are coming here to look around. And that's only wise. Even though this *ménage à trois* is a shotgun marriage, divorce is out of the question. The Americans may refuse or postpone or severely restrict the North American Free Trade Agreement, but Mexico will likely remain an open and receptive place to do business.

Canada and Mexico are economically integrated with the United States — for better or for worse. Some 80 per cent of Canada's exports head south, and 74 per cent of Mexico's head north. And vice versa: the two biggest customers for U.S. goods are Canada and Mexico. The question of whether or not NAFTA will be rejected by Congress is not relevant anymore. It certainly would be a psychological setback for Mexico, but the fact is that *de facto* freer trade already exists with Mexico as a result of its GATT membership and proximity.

The only way Mexico — or Canada — will close its economy is if Canadians elect New Democrats or if Mexicans elect populist politician Cuauhtemoc Cardenas in Mexico (whose father confiscated foreign oil companies in 1938 as Mexico's president). But even the election of anti-trade parties won't change the fact that the *ménage à trois* — with or without a formal NAFTA- is the continent's destiny.

NORTH AMERICA'S BERLIN WALL

Every night at a 10-kilometre stretch of border between California and Mexico, thousands of Mexicans wait for border guards to change shifts. Then, they make a run for it. Accompanied by three tough Mexican secret policemen, a social worker with the Catholic church, and a San Diego photographer, I spent the night there in December 1990. This area was the crossing point into the United States for more than half of Mexican illegals, an average of 3,000 per night.

We met in the police station at midnight, then drove in two trucks to several points on the border. The secret police with us, armed with pistols and rifles, had been deployed by the Mexican government to protect those on the Mexican side of the border from thugs who robbed them of their life's savings or from corrupt police who shook them down before they left.

At 2:30 a.m., the scene was surreal. Stadium lights flooded a one-kilometre no man's land that hundreds intended to run across when the border guards changed shifts. Until that happened, hundreds of Mexican men, women, and children slept or huddled around campfires or tire fires. A lantern glowed in a makeshift cantina where Esperanza Medina sold chocolate bars, Marlboro cigarettes, and hot food and drinks. For 10 cents a night, she'd rent you a discarded car seat and blanket. That night her "motel" was fully booked. Her guests burrowed under blankets to escape the cold, only their blue-jeaned legs and running shoes visible. Awake was a young woman holding her sleeping infant. She smiled. A nearby tunnel under the highway served as a community toilet.

"We call it the Border Inn," cracked a Mexican policeman decked out in a bullet-proof vest and a holstered ornate silver pistol. Of the 3,000 or so Mexicans per night who attempt the border crossing, those who make it to the United States pick fruit and vegetables, wash dishes, pump gas, or do odd jobs. Most return to Mexico occasionally to see loved ones. Many are eventually caught by U.S. officials and deported, only to cross again. Police told me that five out of six will make it past El Buho, "The Owl." Mexicans used this nickname to refer to U.S. border police whose ultra-violet night scopes allowed them to see in the dark. This section of the border, called W-3 South, was the favourite crossing point these days. Another was the more accessible, bone-dry aqueduct along the border, floodlit by tall stadium lights installed last year by U.S. officials. The lights and border-patrol cars gave the area an eerie feel, like an arena for a night-time sports event — one of the world's most desperate footraces.

The U.S.–Mexican border is North America's Berlin Wall and the reason why free trade with Mexico may be inevitable. Like Europe, the United States is the recipient of a deluge of illegal aliens - in the latter case, 1.5 million annually. All attempts to erect an impenetrable Iron Curtain have failed.

In fact, the U.S. Berlin Wall has been a human-rights disgrace. U.S. border police have been allowed to shoot to kill if they believed their lives were endangered. Mexicans were murdered — cases have been documented of Mexicans who were shot in the back — but prosecutions were rare. On November 30, 1990, one Mexican was shot while standing at a fence on Mexican soil. Even when they got past the no man's land, the Mexicans faced vigilantes who shot them, or sprayed them with indelible fluorescent paint. The final obstacle on their dangerous gauntlet run was a deadly freeway where at least one illegal alien was killed per month. Weeks before I came here, a mother and her two toddlers attempting to cross were hit by several cars and died.

Americans argued that the Mexicans must be apprehended because they were breaking the law. But a terrible Catch-22 was in play: Mexican agricultural products were mostly banned from the United States, thanks to the powerful California farm lobby. And yet these same protectionist farmers used illegal Mexican immigrants to pick as much as 65 per cent of their crops. Despite their virtual dependence on a Mexican workforce, U.S. farmers made no move to legitimize the practice by asking the U.S. government to grant a sufficient number of seasonal work permits. Visas would bring with them safety and wage standards, fringe benefits, and paperwork. So the farmers set up protectionist barriers, then encouraged the Mexicans to break the law.

With their products shut out of U.S. stores, Mexicans — like Eastern Europeans — had only themselves to export. Besides, millions were leaving the land every year because of drought, depressed prices (a by-product of the agricultural subsidy war between the United States and Europe), and the destruction of Mexican farmlands by water polluted by pesticides from U.S. farms.

So they ran. With their life savings sewn into their jackets and their babies clutched closely, they ran into the arms of U.S. farmers or other employers who exploited them by paying them less than minimum wage. Sometimes they avoided paying them altogether by turning them over to immigration officers for deportation just before payday.

It is hard for Canadians who also share a long border with Americans to understand what is going on here. Canadians are not brown-skinned and are not leaving their country in droves. What goes on in El Bordo every day of the week is, in part, institutionalized racism.

"Absolutely. This is certainly institutionalized violence. An average of one person is killed per month, mostly at Tijuana," said Rosario Green, executive secretary of Mexico's first independent Human Rights Commission, in Mexico City.

She had just finished investigating a tragic case involving

a Mexican living in Mexico who had a green card entitling him to cross the border daily for work in the United States. One day, a border guard took his papers away from him without explanation and said he would return them within a few days after double-checking their authenticity. The next day, the man had to cross illegally in order to go to work. During that attempt, he was arrested, knocked to the ground, and shot when he tried to get up. "They said he was reaching for a gun when they shot him, but he had no fingers on his right hand. It was deformed," Green said.

Fear of such incidents was not on the minds of two young men — Jose and Pedro — that night in December 1990 while they were joking around near Esperanza's cantina. Mexicans are warm, polite people with ready smiles and generous spirits. "All me and my friends want to do is make $3,000 in the U.S. and come back and start a little business," said Jose. Both 17-year-olds, they were being used by a system that would not legitimize them. The two crossed the U.S. border every week to jobs in San Diego. One was a restaurant dishwasher, the other a janitor. Their employers knew they were illegals, yet deducted taxes from their paycheques and probably pocketed the proceeds. The men could not get immigration papers and knew they would eventually be caught, Jose says, but thus far they had saved nearly enough money to buy a 1972 Ford. Then they would open a taxicab business together in Tijuana.

The United States is in the same boat as Western Europe. Both share sieve-like borders with people whose labour rates are one-tenth or less their own. The correction bringing up low wages and bringing high ones down is already underway.

While Canadians do not identify with what goes on along the U.S.–Mexican border, the situations are not dissimilar:

the overriding attractiveness of the United States has drawn Canadians and Mexicans alike, and given the two countries little policy room to manoeuvre, whether it is in terms of taxes or laws.

AMERICA'S THIRD WORLD

The United States faces not only teeming millions from beyond its borders trying to get in and grab a piece of its prosperity, but also the demands of millions within its borders. America's underclass has been a casualty of the Cold War. Life may have been dreadful in the former Soviet Union, but so was life for many Americans. Both superpowers squandered their wealth on arms, spending money that could have been used to look after the needs of all citizens.

The difference between the two superpowers is that the United States is poised this decade to benefit from the financial savings that will result from its reduced military role. It will also profit from the exploitation of the vast hinterland of the Americas through the formation of an hemispheric trading bloc. And what is good for the United States is good for Canada because our economies are so enmeshed.

Freer trade has benefited the United States mightily since the war by providing cheap imports for its consumers in return for vast new markets for its exports. But the United States is the least dependent upon trade of all industrialized nations. Less than 10 per cent of its entire economic output is earmarked for export as compared with 20 per cent of Canada's. This is the case, in part, because U.S. industries can prosper serving the vast home market alone, where a large population enjoys one of the world's highest disposable incomes. That luxurious position means protectionism is more viable for the United States than, say, for Canada or Luxembourg, where living standards are largely based upon an ability to sell things outside relatively tiny economies. Despite the underlying economic strength of the United States, the U.S. way of life was sustained, as was the Soviet way of life, by a military-industrial complex. Besides weaning itself off defence expenditures, the United States — like the former Soviet Union — has other enormous adjustments to make.

The challenges are the same. America's third-world residents and the Russians have been mistreated and brutalized. In urban centres, both have been forced to live in horrible conditions, crammed into neglected highrises covered in graffiti and grime. Ironically, the Russian poor are better off than their U.S. counterparts because they are not forced to live in dangerous neighbourhoods filled with drug dealers and violent criminals. Crime has become so horrific in Washington, D.C., that in 1990 murder became the leading cause of death among children under 12 years of age.

While most crimes of all kinds in the United States were committed by whites, underclass anger and victimization accounted for much of that nation's shamefully high murder rate. Partly because violence feeds on itself, Americans refuse to legislate sensible gun controls, such as those that exist in most of the rest of the world. The result is a country armed to the teeth. Motorists frequently shoot one another over perceived traffic offences, and neighbours are gunned down during garden spats. Matrimonial slaughter — involving infidelity, alcohol, and ready access to a gun — is commonplace at all socioeconomic levels. In 1992, the Atlanta Center for Disease Control declared that murder in the United States had reached "epidemic" proportions: every 22 minutes, 24 hours a day, 7 days per week, an American is killed.

Other statistics published in 1992 suggested that there would be even more crime casualties in future. A respected think tank reported that 42 per cent of young black men between 18 and 35 years of age in Washington, D.C., were in jail, on bail, wanted, or on parole. In nearby Baltimore, 56 per cent of young black males were under some form of justice restriction. "We're also looking at Philadelphia, Los Angeles, Detroit, Chicago, and others. Initial figures suggest these cities are very much in line — somewhere between 45 and 55 per cent — and the trend is up," announced Jerome G. Miller, spokesman with National Center on Institutions and Alternatives.

Such facts and figures hold disastrous implications for U.S. society and young blacks who are not in trouble with the law. Innocent young men are routinely stopped and searched by police. Others are watched closely in stores by detectives worried about shoplifting, or refused jobs by employers fearful of pilferage. Because black men are subjected to closer scrutiny than white men, a greater proportion of them are caught breaking laws. Once charged with criminal offences, most continue a life of criminal behaviour: ex-convicts are denied employment opportunities and apprentice with criminal mentors while locked behind bars.

Only 8 per cent of youthful crimes in the United States are violent; most of them are drug related. But drug usage often leads to drug trafficking and more serious offences. "The accounts of automatic weapons shoot-outs and turf wars and drive-by killings are not merely stories made up by racists to make African Americans look bad. They happen," wrote black American journalist William Raspberry in

1993.

Conditions in U.S. cities have greatly worsened postwar because of the mass migration of uneducated blacks from the South to unskilled factory jobs and crowded slums in northern cities. In the South, blacks were kept in line by force by segregationists or the Ku-Klux-Klan. Even in the northern cities, blacks faced discrimination from employers, unions, landlords, and governments until the civil-rights movement exploded into the public-policy forefront with a Supreme Court ruling in 1959 which led to the desegregation of schools in Little Rock, Arkansas. This ruling was backed by U.S. army intervention after state officials initially balked at the court's decision. As is true of the advent of any new world "order," there is always an extensive period of painful restructuring. Blacks still haven't achieved equality by a long shot, and growing impatience in cramped conditions has led to violence and criminal behaviour.

America's biggest disgrace is its lack of equalization payments for education. Only a handful of states have adopted this system, which is used in Europe and Canada. The result is uneven publicly funded education and unfair opportunities for wealthy children.

Many high schools in wealthy white suburbs have teachers with doctorates on staff because local taxpayers never refuse to pay increased property taxes if the money is spent on education. Meanwhile, in the ghettos, students are lucky to have access to teachers with degrees. Their schools are dilapidated. They do not offer fancy language laboratories, auditoriums for student performances, or many extracurricular activities. Schools in wealthy suburbs crank out students with high grade-point averages, destined for the country's best colleges. Schools in poor neighbourhoods turn out fewer graduates and fewer kids qualified to enter institutions of higher learning. This unjust difference in the quality of publicly supported education is due to the fact that Americans have no equalization mechanism to spread taxes evenly among schools. Instead, high tax–paying white suburbs deliver first-class education, and poor black neighbourhoods are stuck with fourth-rate schooling.

This inequity has helped perpetuate the disparity between blacks and whites and rich and poor in the United States. It has also ruined America's cities: after the Second World War, whites fled to suburbs and better schools, leaving behind an eroding tax base, deteriorating city infrastructure, and poorly funded schools. The gap is stunning in some states. A white high school in a wealthy New Jersey suburb spends US$14,000 per student per year while the state's average for black kids is only US$4,000 per year. While money isn't everything in education, it certainly helps. And without good education, America's blacks and Hispanics have a tougher time breaking the poverty cycle.

Litigation in several states in the 1980s addressed the injustice, and eventually equalization will be universal. Disenfranchised, economically and educationally, generations of ambitious blacks have been forced to grab opportunities by turning to crime. Women have too many children, often out of wedlock, and plunge themselves into lives of poverty. America's inner cities have become cesspools of criminality, anger, broken dreams, abuse, frustration, and drug usage. As the statistics show, the way out for many young black men is the lawless subculture of drugs, break-ins, thefts, and even murder. Rap music celebrates anarchy and cop killing.

As if to underscore the fact that progress has not been

rapid enough, riots erupted in Los Angeles in 1992 — the worst urban disturbance of the century. A rampage of looting and murder followed the disgraceful acquittal by a white jury of four white policemen videotaped mercilessly beating a black suspect. The verdict sparked full-scale civil disorder, causing $1.2 billion in property damage — more than the San Francisco earthquake. Even more frightening, some 56 persons were murdered during several days of rampage in the city of 3 million (county of 10 million). The 56 victims represented only 3 per cent of that year's murders.

Huge portions of Los Angeles — and other U.S. inner cities — are without adequate, or sometimes any, police protection. In many cities, firefighters and cops routinely refuse to answer calls for help in certain areas where snipers or gangs have murdered their colleagues. Such anarchy, in a society where arms are sold to anyone with a driver's licence, is a guarantee that urban violence will continue. It takes only a few thousand dysfunctional persons to wreak havoc.

Obviously, post–Cold War America has to get more of a grip on itself. Like Western Europe, it faces hordes at its gates. But, unlike Europe, it also faces hordes within its gates. America's social problems are the result of 200 years of brutalization of blacks and a form of subtle racialism that has perpetuated privileges for rich whites at the expense of the poor.

Improvements have been impressive, but much more needs to be done. With the Soviet threat gone, America will become more preoccupied with its own internal crises. And an America less willing to sort out global predicaments means that the United Nations will play a more significant role in the twenty-first century than ever before.

THE NORTH AMERICAN POWERHOUSE

North America will remain the richest, and safest, part of the global economy for a number of important reasons. Its engine of growth — the U.S. economy — is more diversi- fied, advanced, and innovative than Europe's Germany or Asia's Japan. The U.S. economy is larger than those of the two others combined.

The twentieth century has been called the "American cen- tury" because the United States enjoyed two advantages. It was, in essence, ahead of the world in terms of trade oppor- tunities because it was fiercely capitalist and was itself a gigantic common market of 280 million people. The United States was also resource and oil rich, which greatly bene- fited its industries. North American free trade, or hemi- spheric free trade, will do more of the same - provide U.S. capitalists with vast new markets and provide its industries and consumers with plentiful resources and oil. As the United States prospers, so does Canada, Mexico, and the others who will be able to freely export goods, commodities, and services to that wealthy marketplace.

While economic pre-eminence is assured, Americans will face more challenges in terms of sorting out their social prob- lems. But the United States is a mature, responsive democ- racy, and injustices are being addressed. Progress has been rapid, compared with other countries. As recently as the 1960s, racism was rampant throughout the United States; there was no black middle class and few black university graduates. Until the civil-rights movement came along, vio- lence and legalized discrimination against blacks were com- monplace. This is no longer the case.

Of the three Triad members, North America will fare the best for a number of other reasons. First, it is protected by the U.S. military, the world's most powerful. Wars and potential conflicts surround Europe, in Eastern Europe, the Middle East, and North Africa. Asia is plagued with the nagging Cambodian conflict; potential land and border disputes; a dangerous arms build-up; nuclear arms in China, both Koreas, India and Pakistan; and no moral leader in the region with sufficient military strength to keep the peace. The U.S. presence in Japan and South Korea will, in future, become more of a comfort than a guarantee of peace. The United States is unlikely to become involved in another war in Asia after the Vietnam fiasco.

North America will remain safer and more prosperous than other regions of the world in future because it is also the world's most homogeneous trading bloc. There are no religious tensions in the entire hemisphere. Borders are not an issue anywhere. And there are only three major languages - English, Spanish, and Portuguese. (French is spoken only in Quebec and Haiti.) By comparison, the European Community has nine official languages, and dozens more languages and other religions exist beyond its eastern border. The same pluralism exists in Asia. Operating in many languages increases not only the cost of doing business but the likelihood of misunderstandings, political disagreements, and tensions or violence.

EUROPE

IT HAS BEEN APPARENT FOR SOME TIME THAT EUROPE
intends to establish itself as a sort of fortified free-trade
zone, Fortress Europe, enabling it to become a powerful pillar in the international economic triad. This may
yet be the result, but the collapse of the communist
empire has interrupted the process and sparked a massive restructuring and serious recession. Western Europe is in
for a considerable correction, or lowering, of its living standards this decade. The many problems associated with the
communist collapse, including mass migrations of economic
and political refugees, environmental disasters, nationalist
uprisings, and generalized political instability, are going to
preoccupy and weaken Europe for years to come. The phys-
ical dislocation of people whose economic base has been
destroyed is especially devastating in its effects. Waves of
desperate and homeless migrants are no easier to halt in
Europe than they are in the southern United States. If Europe
sees its way to embracing the east, however, and the benefits
of freer trade are shared across the continent, it will be a
powerful economic entity indeed in the next century.

But there is resistance, even in the face of encouraging pronouncements. Treaties with five Eastern-bloc countries, called Europe Agreements, have paid only lip-service to freer trade because trade in agriculture, steel, and textiles — the only activities in which easterners enjoy competitive advantages over westerners — is restricted. Tariffs remain for years, and sudden surges of imports in these areas trigger protectionist measures such as higher tariffs, quotas, or even bans. So far, Europe Agreements with Poland, Czechoslovakia, and Hungary were signed by the European Community in December 1991, and with Rumania and Bulgaria in 1993. No promise has been made to let any of the five into the European Community.

When Czech steel exports to the West jumped by 56 per cent in 1992, and by 31 per cent in Hungary, the EC slapped anti-dumping duties on a number of eastern countries on a number of products. There are calls for environmental dumping categories against eastern polluters to level the playing field against western firms who must bear the cost of running clean operations. Then, in 1993, a hoof-and-mouth outbreak in Yugoslavia led to a total ban on livestock and dairy imports from Eastern Europe. The Czech farm minister reacted angrily, calling the meat ban the "restoration of the iron curtain." The European Bank for Reconstruction and Development in early 1993 called for the Europe Agreements to be scrapped. Similar protectionist measures are to be embodied in the sidebar agreements accompanying the North American Free Trade Agreement. Such bullying is not only bad economics, but worse. Both the European Community and the United States have benefited mightily from surging exports into the newly opened and struggling economies of their neighbours. But both refuse to provide the same access.

To deny access for their products will result in the continuing export of people.

THE OLD IRON CURTAIN

Before the Berlin Wall came down in the fall of 1989, hundreds of thousands of protesters gathered on streets in the
East and chanted: "If the Deutschmark doesn't come to us
we will go to the Deutschmark." And that is precisely what
they did. Thousands of East Germans poured across the border, unimpeded by the Russian troops and border guards
who formerly had barred the way. During those days of
protest and disruption, East German industry virtually
ground to a halt, and West German cities reeled under the
assault of the thousands of homeless refugees who landed
on their doorstep, requiring food, clothing, shelter, schooling,
medical attention, and welfare.

Paradoxically, West German politicians had to absorb
East Germany into their economy in order to keep East
Germans at home. The benefits of Western capitalism had to
be made available where they lived or the people would
come looking for them. On July 1, 1990, less than one year
after the dramatic collapse of communism, unification was
accomplished.

"Once the wall came down the process was out of control," explained Professor Kurt Biedenkopf, former president of the ruling Christian Democrats, in an interview in
May 1990. "Once the wall came down, there was no discretion. We already had unity. The elimination of the wall is
unity. Not everyone understood that. The only way to stop
unity is to put the wall back."

In fact, the unification of the two Germanys did not stop the migration from Eastern Europe. By 1993, Germany and other front-line countries along the former Iron Curtain boundary had been invaded by millions of illegal aliens. Austria deployed its army to guard the full length of its border. So did the Czechs, Swiss, and Italians. A new Iron Curtain formed. Austrian soldiers with Uzi submachine-guns patrolled the line, while armed helicopters, floodlights glaring, hovered over forests and river crossings at night.

Such efforts rarely worked. Rumours would sweep a city or even country, and thousands would migrate all at once. In 1990, Italy, for instance, suddenly received 30,000 uninvited Albanians who had captured ships and ordered their crews to sail for Italy, just a few hours away. In the summer of 1992, another 30,000 Albanians living in Kosovo feared a Serbian invasion and ethnic cleansing. They arrived en masse in Sweden.

A TALE OF TWO CAR PLANTS

General Motors' Adam Opel AG's auto plant in Rüsselsheim, outside Frankfurt, was state of the art. One of the world's most computerized and robotized plants, it spat out different models, one after another. A van with right-hand drive would be followed by a sedan with steering on the left-hand side. Production was accomplished largely by computers with electronic eyes, and was far cheaper to operate than assembly run by people. By 1990, the resistance of the community and a shortage of land had made expansion at that plant impossible, so the company was looking around for new production facilities at another location. The obvious solution — from the point of view of the German government's privatization agency — was for Opel to buy and renovate one of East Germany's car makers.

The government agency favoured Automobile Verken Eisenach. Some six hours away from Rüsselsheim by car, the Eisenach company employed 10,000 workers to manufacture the Wartburg, a fume-belching vehicle unsaleable to Westerners. Opel inspected the premises and was horrified by what it saw. The technology used was 40 years behind the times. In Opel's judgment, the East German workers were inefficient and had poor work habits. If parts were not delivered, the entire factory often would shut down and the workers would drift home — sometimes for days. Adam Opel's 17,500 workers and 262 robots produced 1,400 cars a day. Meanwhile, "in Eisenach, a workforce of 10,000 makes 250 lousy cars a day," explained Opel spokesman Helmut Verthake. "Their cars are prewar standard. There is an assembly line, but no marketing, and they have made the same model for 40 years. Deliveries take 13 years and people had to pay cash up front. When we send people there to work, they must sleep in their cars. There are no hotels and no restaurants. There is nothing at Eisenach. You might as well burn it down and start over again."

Not surprisingly, Opel turned down the chance to take over the East German facilities. Eventually the company bought half of Sweden's Saab-Scania AB, and expanded production to Saab's modern, but underutilized plants, in Europe. Similarly, Volkswagen leapfrogged East Germany and bought 30 per cent of Czechoslovakia's auto maker Skoda.

These two examples reveal why German industrialists have avoided East Germany. Another factor in their decision was Chancellor Helmut Kohl's promise to West German unions that they would have wage parity with East German workers by 1994. That decision single-handedly escalated the cost of unification by removing any advantage East Germany might have enjoyed in attracting investment in its manufacturing sector. This effectively condemned the inefficient, unautomated East German workers to unemployment. As their wages marched toward parity with their automated western counterparts, they became less competitive. Industrialists avoided East Germany and concentrated on new investments and plants in Czechoslovakia, Poland, and elsewhere. So Germany was unable to attract private-sector investment to rebuild the East, which in turn meant that German taxpayers were obliged either to support unemployed workers or to subsidize East Germany's industrial white elephants.

In an interview in January 1993, in *The Financial Post*, Germany's most powerful bureaucrat, Hans Teitmayer of the Bundesbank, cited wage parity as Germany's principal economic problem. His figures showed that, by the end of 1992, East German workers were earning 70 per cent of the wages paid to their West German counterparts, and deserved half that much. In early 1993, as the government in Bonn talked of slowing down wage hikes, East and West German unionists marched by the thousands in the streets throughout the country in protest. Business ground to a halt in scores of cities as workers laid down tools in a massive show of disgust at broken political promises of wage parity.

THE DELUGE

In May 1990, just months after the wall came down, the tree-lined boulevard leading to the Brandenburg Gate in Berlin was lined with dozens of beat-up buses from Poland. Bus entrepreneurs drove through the night so their passengers could buy cans of peaches, ghetto-blasters, car parts, and other products to take home for resale or their own use. For years, Poland's communist regime had allowed open-air farmers' markets. Such commerce had created an entrepreneurial culture in Poland, and tens of thousands of Poles were well versed in how to hustle to make a living.

Besides Poles, Germany's parks were filled with homeless refugees, many from Rumania. They slept under the stars, took shelter in doorways, and defecated in alleys. They were in evidence by day along Berlin's fashionable boulevards. There, outside the outdoor cafés, quartets played gypsy melodies and passed Burger King containers for donations. In May 1990, on Berlin's street corners, mothers clutched their babies and begged for money from passers-by.

But the Germans were making money. Off Berlin's main street was a district dubbed "Polish Paradise." Queues of Poles in cheap clothes formed outside discount shops and loaded their cargo into buses or cars. They returned week after week. Many eventually made wholesale connections themselves.

Elsewhere in Europe the new entrepreneurs made their presence known. Old cars and buses filled with Hungarians and Poles toured Western Europe. Sometimes they would set up shop at the side of the road, and sell everything from live hogs to bottled jams, pickles, and sausages in open contravention of Europe's monopolistic and subsidized farm policies. Sometimes there were scuffles, arrests, and deportations. Europe's black market flourished.

These acts of commercial piracy underscored just how untenable Fortress Europe was. With wages in the east so much lower than those in the west, Eastern Europeans could undercut western competitors by a healthy margin. Blocked by the west, they were forced to smuggle and sell illegally into the market. Some exported themselves.

Policies to keep them and their products out simply stalled the inevitable. The collapse of the communist empire meant that 400 million Eastern Europeans had to find a way to make a living. One way or another, they would join the global economy. Europe as a whole was facing the same decision Germany had been confronted with when the Berlin Wall was dismantled. As Biedenkopf said: "Once the wall came down, it was out of control. We already had unity."

But even as late as 1993, Western European politicians preferred to believe that the burgeoning, anarchic economy of the east could be ignored. Eastern products were still kept out of the west. There was no consensus in Brussels, except that the European Community itself should integrate as quickly as possible. Britain and Germany argued that Central Europe and the three Baltic states should be absorbed into the EC without delay. Others, led by protectionist France, resisted. Underlying Europe's divisions was the fact that all member countries were instinctively protectionist, unwilling to open their heavily subsidized and inefficient markets to any competition.

In the absence of enlightened trade policies, Western European countries became involuntary hosts to about one million uninvited Eastern European immigrants each year after the Cold War ended. For the first time in history, by 1992, Western European countries surpassed, as immigration havens, the world's four traditional destinations: Canada, the United States, Australia, and New Zealand. U.N. officials in Geneva, Switzerland, said the immigration could accelerate. Their biggest fear was that once former Soviet residents were given passports, millions would bolt for the west to improve their opportunities. Worse, according to U.N. refugee expert Jonas Widgren, if anarchy set in, or even several Yugoslav-scale conflicts occurred at once, Europe could be in for "an apocalyptic migration of 10 million or more annually."

By 1992, Widgren's prophecy had partially come true, as Germany was absorbing 500,000 refugees per year into its economy — twice as many as in 1991 and five times the number absorbed in 1988. It also represented 60 per cent of Europe's total, and an annual expense of DM15,000 per refugee. That burden, plus the inordinately high cost of unification, led to protest and violence by 1992. At a rally attended by 300,000 Germans on November 8, 1992, to decry the refugee incursion, the once-popular Chancellor Kohl was pelted with eggs, paint, and fruit. Left-wing and right-wing rowdies alike drowned out his remarks, but there was no end in sight.

Discussions to amend Germany's constitution in order to address the immigration problem reached an impasse. At issue was a guarantee of citizenship to anyone of German extraction, plus the amendment forbidding German soldiers to serve outside German boundaries. Hard-liners argued that ethnic citizenship must be erased to avert the possibility that some 12 million German ethnics might claim German citizenship when Soviet borders were opened. They also argued that German troops must be deployed to fortify the borders and to assist in ending the civil war in the Balkans. Like the Japanese, the Germans fear that the rise of their military again may lead them to another devastating war. The government has chosen, instead, to offer financial assistance so that others could do the dirty work in Yugoslavia or the Gulf.

HORDES AT THE GATE

The U.N. Human Rights Commission's headquarters in Geneva, Switzerland, sprawls along the shores of gentle Lake Geneva, Europe's second-largest body of fresh water. Geneva's luxury hotels are normally the habitat of the rich and famous but, in August 1992, they housed hundreds of refugees who had fled Yugoslavia's violence. The Swiss government had no housing available for the latest arrivals and, in emergencies, put them up in hotel rooms that cost as much as US$500 a night. Of course, most refugees were housed in temporary holding areas like one in a barracks near Geneva's spanking-new international airport. There, 50 Eastern European and Sri Lankan refugee families awaited apartments, welfare payments, schools, and other entitlements from the besieged Swiss government.

Besides the east-west migration, nearly 2 million people have been made homeless by Yugoslavia's civil wars. They are a special case, one hopes temporary, but European countries also have suffered from those taking advantage of the U.N. Convention on Refugees. Countries that have signed the convention agreed to feed, house, and protect anyone who arrives at their borders and declares himself or herself to be a refugee. The spirit of the convention is to protect people from politically motivated injustice and abuse.

But migrants are often opportunists who, when investigated by refugee authorities, are found to have been spurred on by economic rather than political factors. Canada, the United States, and Europe have rules allowing the deportation of persons posing as political refugees, but deportations are subject to appeal and take years to put into effect. Often, by the time a deportation is upheld in the courts, the guilty party has disappeared.

This loop hole, through which millions around the world have passed, has given rise, not surprisingly, to an industry. Advisers who help people get into foreign countries are called "shleppers" in Eastern Europe; in the Far East, they are known as "snakeheads"; and in Latin America, as "coyotes." The current price for getting someone into North America from Sri Lanka or the Middle East is roughly US$5,000 and includes instructions, contact names at the destination country, and fake documentation. Also provided is guidance on how to claim political-refugee status and what entitlements the target country has to offer. In Canada, for instance, political refugees are housed, fed, clothed, and given welfare. One Toronto welfare worker said bogus political refugees arriving in the city were actually given phone numbers by their "advisers" for local welfare offices where their native tongue was spoken. They would call from payphones in the airport to set up appointments.

Because of such migration, it has been estimated that, in 1993, overcrowded Western Europe now has a shortage of 1.5 million apartments. The effect of unwanted immigrants on small countries has been dramatic. After the Iron Curtain fell, Sweden received some 300 Rumanians per day. Some were sent back, and the flow stopped temporarily. Then, within a few days, in the summer of 1992, about 30,000 ethnic Albanians landed in Sweden. They had travelled from Kosovo, a city inside Macedonia, fearing "ethnic cleansing" by Serbian armies. When she was asked how they decided to go to Sweden and how they got there, U.N. refugee spokesperson Irene Kahn said: "Easy. They walked to Poland and took the ferry to Sweden. By the thousands."

Similarly, tiny Switzerland with a population of only 6.6 million people, absorbed 30,000 refugees a year in 1991 and 1992 — twice as many as Canada, with a population of 27 million, had taken in. While the Swiss and Swedes could absorb the cost, those bearing the brunt — countries adjacent to, or involved in, the violence in Yugoslavia — were certainly not in any financial condition to do so. Of the 1.8 million displaced persons in 1992, Bosnia-Herzegovina itself had hundreds of thousands of refugees from Serbia and elsewhere; Serbia had 400,000; Croatia, 600,000; Slovenia, 300,000; and Hungary, 60,000.

"This is a different kind of war in Yugoslavia," said U.N. official Irene Kahn. "Like other wars, it causes dislocation of people as a side-effect, but the ethnic cleansing in Yugoslavia is actually aimed at dislocating people. So far, 2.6 million people are in need and getting assistance, with 1.9 million truly displaced and living in hotels, schools, or barracks."

The costs were staggering. In early 1992, the U.N.'s Yugoslav budget was $160 million. By fall 1992, with three times as many displaced persons as had been anticipated, the cost swelled to $600 million. While that expense was shared among U.N. members, officials pointed out that Western Europe was bearing the additional expense of absorbing Yugoslav immigrants.

There were fears that the bloodshed would spread throughout the Balkans and into the former Soviet Union as old borders were replaced with ones drawn along linguistic, religious, or ethnic lines. Dozens of cease-fire agreements negotiated by the European Community were ignored, and in 1992 U.N. peacekeeping forces were deployed to get food through to the dispossessed. But it was apparent that the Balkans could become the continent's Northern Ireland: the site of chronic unrest and violence — expensive, insoluble.

An interesting aspect about the war in Yugoslavia was the reluctance of the United States — even under former president George Bush — to send troops to curb the Serbians, even though they were simply a Slavic version of Saddam Hussein's Iraqi army. Invasions of independent republics, death camps, violence, and indications that widespread rape had occurred were more than sufficient reason to bomb the Serbs in their homes. Even so, hundreds of thousands of idle U.S. troops remained safe in their military bases in Germany, just a few hundred kilometres away.

This situation underscored the fact that the United States would no longer protect Europe from European problems. For decades, Western European nations had enjoyed the protection of a generous United States and spent their own money creating a welfare state. The German constitution, and the European failure to ratify the Maastricht Treaty, were impediments to any form of unified, sizeable initiative. Europe's 12 countries still had 12 foreign policies, and Germany, like Japan, was frightened of changing its pacifist constitution to allow German soldiers to leave its soil. Other European countries were frightened of the same possibility. Sooner or later, Europe will certainly have to accept responsibility for maintaining peace within its boundaries, even if it means combining to form a single pan-European military force. This eventuality is not contained in the Maastricht Treaty but is clearly desired in Brussels.

CENTRAL EUROPE'S SUCCESS STORIES

Tom Bata is a legend in Czechoslovakia. He fled the country just hours ahead of the Nazi invasion and rebuilt his family's shoe empire in Canada and in 60 countries around the world. During his "exile" in Canada, Bata often spoke out against communism on Radio Free Europe, and tape cassettes bearing the same message were smuggled into the country. President Vaclav Havel's grandfather worked for Bata's father, as did many other prominent Czechs, which is why, within days of Havel's Velvet Revolution, in November 1989, Bata was invited to come home. He and his Swiss-born wife, Sonja, returned in December 1989 to a hero's welcome.

"I remember we were on the jet, entering Czech airspace, and the pilot asked Tom to come forward to listen to the air traffic controller in Prague. The man said, 'Welcome home Mr. Bata.' It was quite touching," recalled Sonja. "Just before we landed, we saw thousands of people on the airfield and wondered what had happened and whether we could land. But they were there for Tom."

Expatriates like Bata play an important role — often merely symbolic — in terms of helping turn around Eastern Europe. But such entrepreneurs can help in only small ways. It is hard to quantify how many expats have invested and how sizeable this type of ethnic investing has been so far. What is really needed to avert the continuing, and expensive, migration of people is a massive Marshall Plan by

Western Europeans - a combined package of financial aid and trade access. As West Germany realized, the only way to keep the easterners at home was to provide them with opportunities and expertise there.

This is what the Batas are attempting to do. They have invested themselves, but have also contributed to the rebuilding of the Czech economy by encouraging others to invest in Czech industry. I visited Bata's newly acquired shoe factory, some 25 kilometres from Zlin. The Batas invested $2.4 million here, mostly to create a prototype plant for Czechs to study. Rows of women operated sewing machines in a plant made bright and cheerful by the first fresh coat of paint it had worn in decades. Despite a low living standard, wages and fringe benefits combined to make Czech labour costs in real terms the same as Portugal's, said Sonja. Portugal's labour costs are lower than most in Western Europe, but the fact that Czech rates are, in real terms, nearly as high as those in some Western countries reveals how inefficient they are. Labour-intensive products like shoes should be made in countries like China, say the Batas, where labour costs are a fraction of Czech, Portuguese, or Canadian wage rates. Despite Czech inefficiencies, the Batas have a factory here for emotional reasons.

Retailing in Czechoslovakia is a good news/bad news proposition. Business is booming. There are only 52 shoe stores in all of Prague (with a population of one million) - the number of shoe stores in two large shopping malls in Canada.

By August 1992, sales in Bata's 38 Czech stores outpaced all his other Western European stores, in terms of pairs sold per store. But the retail environment is difficult. Profits made on cheaply priced shoes were considerably lower than in the

West. And laws left over from communist days require retailers to extend a warranty on any product for six months. In the first few months, Bata stores had 10 per cent of the shoes they sold returned for refund or replacement. "They buy leather high heels from Italy and ruin them in a week on Prague's cobblestone streets," said Sonja. So the Bata factory now is making only sturdy shoes for the Czech market.

Bata's managers greeted us at the factory door. Parachuted in from other Bata operations around the world, they had been given the task of changing production methods and training employees. When they arrived, they found manufacturing methods that were inefficient, equipment that was out of date; and a work ethic, as in all socialist countries, that was unacceptable. Workers made only $150 a month, but at any given time 80 of the 600 workers were on maternity leave of up to two years at full pay, a burdensome benefit.

The Bata's newly acquired factory had never been owned by the family, but was built by the communists. The original family enterprise Bata had left behind during the war had been renamed Svit. "The new government would have given the old family enterprise to me for nothing, but I refused. It's a white elephant. No, it's a black elephant," he said as we drove to Svit's headquarters.

Housed in 45 factories, Svit was spewing out 20 million pairs of mediocre shoes a year for Eastern-bloc and Soviet markets. By 1992, not one pair of shoes was being sold to a now-bankrupt Russia. Fortunately, if tragically, the plant was being kept busy by the civil war in Yugoslavia, which had shut down shoe factories that had previously supplied the German market. "Two years ago, Russia was 37 per cent of our sales," explained Svit's general manager, Vladimir

Lukavsky. "Last year [1991], 25 per cent of our production was exported there, but they didn't pay. This year, we will export nothing there."

Sales should hit roughly $240 million this year, but the transition has proven difficult. The Russians used to order 30,000 pairs per style at a crack. In the West, a large order is 3,000 pairs, with style and colour options galore, and fitting and size requirements that greatly tax Lukavsky's workforce. They never had competitors or fussy customers before.

We drank tea in Lukavsky's office because Bata wanted to discuss the possibility that Svit supply shoes for Bata's retail chain. "Nineteen of the 20 directors of Svit have been pushed out, and the company has been split into divisions for purchase by foreigners. I'm optimistic. The workers are becoming more efficient. It is not only a question of age. Some workers who are 55 years of age are more flexible than 17-year-olds. Changes are not going as quickly as I would like, but it is happening," says Lukavsky.

What does it feel like, I asked Lukavsky, to be running a conglomerate that really belongs to Mr. Bata, who's sitting here beside you?

"I haven't thought about it," he replied, to which Bata responded, "I'm glad he's running it and not me."

PRIVATIZATION, CZECH-STYLE

The effort mounted by the Czech government to privatize previously public companies is unique. In August 1992, I visited a Canadian friend, Mart Bakal, a lawyer originally from Winnipeg, who obtained millions of dollars' worth of grants from the U.S. government to set up an investment-evaluation outfit for the Czech government. Since 1991, he has employed several dozen high-priced investment bankers to fetch the highest possible price and the best possible terms from foreigners for Czech assets. Bakal also convinced four top-notch U.S. law firms to lend their services, *pro bono*, in three-month stints. These volunteers line up to help out in order to prospect for future business.

"Our job is to even the playing field for the Czechs," said Bakal, who left Canada for New York City in 1986. "This is very important. The potential buyers come with their Western banks and Western lawyers. Some of them say, 'Boy am I going to beat them up.' We make sure they don't. We try to improve the deal for the government, then it must be approved by the Ministry of Privatization approvals committee."

Germans bought 50 per cent of privatized assets, the Americans 25 per cent, and other Europeans the rest. The Japanese are conspicuously absent. "They are standing back and only want to sell their products here," surmised Bakal. "They don't want to own factories. Maybe someday."

Deals are complicated and take time. "We had three people on the US$414 million Philip Morris purchase of Czech tobacco company Tabak. We had two stages of competitive tenders on that one," he said. Modelled along the lines of Investment Canada, Bakal's advisory group looks after the long-term interests of their citizens when privatizing. They require that foreigners reinvest dividends, make job guarantees, provide retraining and technology transfers, invest more capital, and protect the environment. Fines and deadlines are often built into contracts. Buyers can negotiate terms under whatever legal system they desire.

These deals are necessary; otherwise, the Czechs would

be taken advantage of by westerners in terms of price. Not only that, but the Czechs are denied worker mobility or total trade access to Europe, which means that, without job guarantees, some Western European companies might simply buy a Czech rival, close it, and export their products from their existing facilities in the west. In other words, the Czechs deserve something in return for granting "franchises" or access to their market.

Besides selling large businesses, the Czechs have also aggressively auctioned off small and medium-sized enterprises every Saturday since 1992. Buyers were entitled to government loans to finance their inventories, pay salaries, and make capital improvements. So far, the results are highly visible and successful. Just two years after the Velvet Revolution, Prague has gone from a drab, crumbling city to one with outdoor cafés, brightly painted façades, and stores filled with Western goods. On famed Wenceslaus Square, a Bata shoe store occupies a prime corner, two McDonald's outlets do booming business, and a Kmart occupies centre-block. At the same time as the giants move in, small Czech entrepreneurs use government loans to compete, opening up cafés, nightclubs, newsstands, and convenience stores. Without such loans, western chains would control the country in no time, as Czech citizens have no capital and no expertise yet.

The principal benefit of Czech prime minister Vaclav Klaus's mass privatizations, loans to start small businesses, and a clever voucher system is that it has transformed the country without the sorts of problems that Poland, for example, has experienced — high inflation and high unemployment. The Czechs had already sold to foreigners 1,440 large businesses by 1992. Another 241,000 small and medium-sized businesses had been privatized, and entrepreneurship flourished, fed by income from exports and tourism. A staggering 42 million tourists visited Prague in 1991, partly because it is the only medieval city in Eastern Europe that was left untouched during the Second World War. The fact that it is a medieval city was not sufficient in itself to attract that many visitors when it was under communist rule, so something has changed to make the city even more attractive.

For breweries, hotels, and other assets the government wanted to keep Czech-owned, and for those that remained unsold, Klaus invented a voucher system. Companies were converted into stock-exchange listed companies, and in 1992 every Czech citizen over 18 years of age could buy $300 worth of vouchers. Then, later that year, the government established stock prices for certain companies and published them, plus financial details, in local newspapers. Czechs could swap their vouchers for an equivalent amount of stock in companies they desired. If stock was available, they would get some. If there were more buyers than stock available, all applications were rejected and the stock was reposted at a higher price until desire matched supply. His voucher system was a primitive version of the stock market.

Some privatizations involved a combination of foreign ownership to get capital and know-how plus voucher ownership to let Czechs participate. Volkswagen's $1-billion investment in Czech auto maker Skoda is a case in point. Voucher holders, or shareholders, own 30 per cent of the company. Volkswagen and the government share the rest.

Besides the Czechs and former East Germans, the Poles and Hungarians are on their way toward prosperity. Still struggling are the Slovaks, Rumanians, Bulgarians, and Albanians. And the eight new countries that formerly comprised Yugoslavia are at war or totally paralysed.

Reforms vary and success is uneven. Hungary had a head start, gradually reforming its society after 1969 under the Russians' nose. By the time the curtain fell, the Hungarians had a mixed economy, nicknamed "goulash communism." Still gradualist and heavily in debt, they now have "goulash capitalism," and are rapidly falling behind the Czechs and Poles.

The Poles and Czechs have been the most successful, perhaps because they have a strong sense of national identity and were led out of the communist system by national heroes - Lech Walesa and Vaclav Havel. Perhaps it could be said that the Poles had a head start because they were allowed to travel during the 1980s. In addition, Polish farms were privatized under communism, and open-air markets for agricultural products taught a generation about capitalism. Enterprising farmers and 1.6 million small businesses made up the backbone of the reformed Polish economy. The Polish road to reform, embarked upon in 1989, was brutal. Called the "Cold Shower" treatment, it consisted of decontrolling prices, privatizing enterprise, and selling government assets.

Initially it was a disaster. The size of the economy shrank 11.5 per cent as Soviet markets for heavy industrial production disappeared. Inflation hit 586 per cent. People worried that unemployment would hit 30 per cent in heavy industry, but in fact it hit only 13 per cent. Small enterprises mopped up 12 per cent of the workforce by creating 2 million new jobs.

By 1993, inflation fell to around 30 per cent, and Poland enjoyed a trade surplus with the rest of the world of several billion dollars. As inflation fell and the currency strengthened, foreign investors got involved and started 200,000

private companies and invested in 7,600 existing ones. Italy's
Fiat announced a $2-billion investment in car production
in 1992. A year later, an estimated 60 per cent of Poles
worked in the private sector and accounted for 45 per cent
of the country's GDP. Even more impressive, Poland's economy grew despite four prime ministers and four finance ministers in as many years, and many strikes.

"Poland's efforts to reshape its economy are working,"
crowed *The Economist* in January 1993, "but not always
in the way the reformers intended. Other ex-communist
countries please note."

EUROPE'S CHALLENGE

Like West Germany, Western Europe must eventually inte-
grate with its eastern neighbours. But they are doing everything they can to avoid it. Instead, the 12 rich European
Community countries and their 6 associate members
(Sweden, Norway, Finland, Iceland, Switzerland, and
Austria) have been preoccupied with trying to get the 1992
Maastricht Treaty approved. The treaty — unsigned by
Britain and Denmark when it took effect January 1, 1993
— was designed to create a single economy and single currency. Of more urgency — but not even on the agenda —
was a European army and common foreign policy to tackle
the continent's problems of illegal migration, the Soviet economic collapse, environmental problems, and the war in
Yugoslavia.

During 1992 and 1993, Europe remained frozen at the
switch regarding Yugoslavia. Dozens of cease-fires were
negotiated by Europe, only to be ignored. The European

Community's recognition of Bosnia as a sovereign nation was ignored by Serbian aggressors, and Europe's failure to sort out the partitioning of that fledgling nation was an admission of its weakness. An American offer to strategically bomb the Serbs to end the Bosnian bloodshed if Europe provided ground troops was politely rejected by the Europeans, at odds over what to do in the Balkans. Instead, the United Nations has babysat the war without taking sides.

Europeans are unwilling to realize that they must do what the Germans did after the Berlin Wall came down — merge in an orderly fashion with the east, whether doing so is desirable or not. The fact is, east and west are slowly integrating anyway, which has caused the collapse of Europe's excessive property prices. London houses fetching £200,000 in 1988 fell to £100,000 by 1992, if a buyer could be found. London — touted as Europe's future financial capital — struggled with half-empty office blocks and the bankruptcy of the Canary Wharf project, a white elephant of enormous proportions. Economic activity, meanwhile, shifted eastward. Property values soared in Czechoslovakia, Poland, and Hungary.

The bottom line was that Fortress Europe, with its excessive social benefits and unionism, was in trouble. Even so, European governments dithered, balking at rapid integration because the absorption of East Germany by West Germany had been so badly mishandled. Chancellor Helmut Kohl's excessive generosity to East Germans had resulted in high taxes and interest rates. By 1992, Germany had dragged Europe as a whole into a debilitating recession. Germany — once a lender — began to compete on debt markets to borrow money. Estimates were that it would cost Germany DM100 billion per year for the rest of the century to rebuild

East Germany and support its unemployed and its inefficient industries. This effort would use up all of Germany's
expected investment and trade surpluses.

Another cost to Germany was its attempt to prop up
Mikhail Gorbachev and the Soviet Union. Kohl's government lent the Soviets US$40 billion out of the US$60 billion the Soviets obtained, and pressured other governments
to help out, too. Now that the Soviet Union has fallen apart,
Germany and the other lenders have been left holding the
bag. Worse yet, Germany faced an enormous influx of
German ethnic refugees from the former Soviet Union once
passports were allowed: under Germany's constitution, these
people can claim full German citizenship and privileges.
There may be as many as 6 million German ethnics in the
former Soviet republics.

German extravagance damaged the world economy too.
As Germany began to borrow, not lend, money, it placed
upward pressure on interest rates globally. Its preoccupa-
tion with its new financial burden also contributed to the
GATT impasse over the issue of agricultural subsidies. Thirty
per cent of East Germany's population still lives on inefficient farms, a problem that West Germany now shares. With
unemployment high in the cities of the east, Germany needs
to perpetuate Europe's excessive agricultural subsidies to
help pay the cost of unification, so, uncharacteristically, it
sided with France — and against the United States — on the
issue of farm subsidies. The Americans and their grain-grow-
ing allies balked, GATT negotiations stalled, and subsidies
continued to drive down prices worldwide.

Europe is embattled. The Danes rejected the Maastricht
Treaty, then passed a revised version in mid-1993. Britain's
backbenchers staged open revolts, and many pledged to vote

against the treaty. Leaders everywhere were unpopular, blamed for economic problems beyond anyone's control. Italy erupted after two courageous judges were assassinated by gangsters. Five ministers and Socialist Party leader Benedetto Craxi resigned. Bribery and mafia links were so pervasive that even Giulio Andreotti, seven times prime minister of the country, was accused of having maintained intimate links with organized crime, and magistrates asked parliament to lift his immunity. The exchange-rate mechanism collapsed under German weight in the fall of 1992, wrecking the currencies of Sweden, Norway, Italy, Spain, Britain, and Finland at a cost to their central banks of billions of dollars in reserves. Scandals among British royalty contributed to the destabilization of the pound and the British economy. In 1993, some polls showed for the first time that a majority of Britons questioned the desirability of having a monarchy at all. Lacking a written constitution, Great Britain would have to devise one, and the ownership of North Sea oil and gas resources would be up for grabs, with at least half of it claimed by Scottish sovereigntists. The Swiss elected not to join the European Community.

But Europe will hang together, joined by necessity and subsidies. By 1992, eight EC countries were directly subsidized by Germany, Britain, France, and Holland, and grants were increased to get them to sign the Maastricht Treaty. Annual subsidies to Luxembourg totalled US$1,897 per person; to Ireland, US$678; to Greece, US$375; to Belgium, US$165; to Portugal, US$104; to Denmark, US$97; to Spain, US$73; and to Italy, US$10. The Dutch contributed US$7 per person; the British, US$52; French, US$26; and the Germans, US$140. On top of those subsidies were agricultural ones. Every European paid US$400 more per year for groceries than they would have without subsidies.

With such bribes in place by January 1, 1993, Europe formed a customs union, the first step in the Maastricht process. Eventually a single currency will be adopted. But Europeans — inefficient and protectionist, bogged down by unrealistic, dictatorial labour unions and farmers, and in the absence of an overall increase in the number of jobs in the 1980s — engaged in futile efforts to postpone the inevitable.

Fortress Europe has been under siege, facing the greatest migratory onslaught from the east since the invasion of the Visigoths and Vandals. The Western Europeans, like Canadians, must dismantle their burdensome welfare and political systems to be competitive and retain their living standards. Potentially, and in the long run, free-trade and economic integration across Europe could turn the continent into the world's biggest and richest free-trade zone. Eastern Europeans are aggressive, educated, technologically advanced, and resource-rich. But if the European Community mishandles the situation, they will isolate the east, causing poverty, a possible relapse to communism in some countries, and more Yugoslavias. Western and Eastern Europe share a destiny, whether they want to or not.

THE FAR EAST

ORMER PRESIDENT JIMMY CARTER'S FOREIGN AFFAIRS
adviser, Zbigniew Brzezinski, related a story about
President Carter lecturing China strongman Deng
Xiaoping, back in the 1970s, about human rights.
"Deng asked: 'Does human rights include the freedom of movement?'" recalled Brzezinski. "President
Carter replied, 'Yes,' and Deng said, 'Well, you can have 10
million Chinese tomorrow.' The president changed the subject."

The anecdote illustrated how China's enormous population was not only a burden, but also a weapon in modern-
day geopolitics. The spectre of China's instability and the
threat of a mass migration greater than that Western Europe
faced after the collapse of the Soviet Empire had Asians worried. Deng played on those fears. So would future Chinese
leaders.

If its growth is mishandled, China has a lot to lose. The
region has enjoyed relative peace for two generations, and its
economy, collectively, has become as large as North
America's, generating 22 per cent of the world's gross

national product. Japan's GNP accounts for 70 per cent of Asia's total.

But the driving force in this region — outpacing both Europe and the United States or Canada — is the Chinese "nation," comprising several different sovereign nations or city-states, such as Singapore and Hong Kong. This development seems only appropriate since nearly one out of every four human beings on the planet is Chinese. Even so, it is interesting, and surprising. For hundreds of years, the Chinese people have been conquered, divided, exploited by foreigners, embroiled in civil wars, and impoverished. Now it appears that China and its Far East neighbours will be the driving force in the evolving global economy, outpacing and outgrowing Triad rivals Europe and North America. Already, Asians have challenged Western supremacy in areas such as electronics and automobiles. But besides that, their prosperity is resulting in newfound riches for residents in the region, which, in turn, is creating a vast, local market for exports from within and without Asia.

Clearly — as Deng astutely pointed out to Carter — politicians, both in the East and in the West, cannot, and should not, always have their way. It is the dictates of the marketplace, demographics, the implacable drive to relative economic equality, and desire among human beings to enjoy the best life materially that they can that determines history, and not politics.

But politicians can spoil and interrupt the pursuit of comfort. And Asia is still potentially troublesome. Seven of the world's 12 biggest arms buyers are there, in response to land disputes and fears of a destabilized China or a re-armed Japan. Worse yet, there is no moral or military leadership in the region because the Japanese do not want it, and because Japan is hated and feared by the rest. Asia's is an uneasy peace, kept by an increasingly reluctant United States, with troops in South Korea and Japan and naval bases throughout the Pacific.

Fortunately, the region is still preoccupied with making money, not war. Deng has quietly pulled off the type of dramatic and beneficial economic reforms that some Russians only dream of. Billions of dollars are being poured into manufacturing and technology in China by U.S., European, and Asian investors. Money flows actually increased after the June 4, 1989, massacre at Beijing's Tiananmen Square. While such murderous acts can never be condoned, many of China's neighbours secretly hope that Beijing keeps control.

So far, China has pulled off the seemingly impossible: it has maintained order and also extended more freedoms to its people than they have ever before enjoyed. Should this continue, prosperity in Asia will as well. If it does not, the region — and the world economy — will suffer greatly. A catastrophe in one part of the world now affects the stock markets, trade, and employment in other parts because of the interdependence in a global economy. Germany's recession pulled Europe into recession, and the same effect occurred as the U.S. slowdown brought Canada down with it.

SHENZHEN

The train journey from Hong Kong to Shenzhen takes roughly half an hour. The territory of Hong Kong is a strange mixture of Manhattan-style high-density and deserted, snake-infested hills. But, as the train enters China, the buildings become shabby. Shenzhen's station is decrepit, the border guards' uniforms are ill fitting, and the people were poorly dressed. As it is still a police state, visitors have to present their visas to immigration, fill in an AIDS form at the health department (visitors are subject to random blood tests), and pass through customs. Beyond the officials, the train station is filled with shops selling cigarettes and souvenirs in distinctly uninviting, grey surroundings.

Outside, the new city of Shenzhen is like a treeless construction site. Erection cranes are everywhere. So is scaffolding 20 storeys high, made out of bamboo. Billboards everywhere advertise Western and Japanese goods. People bustle, vendors hustle. This is truly the Klondike in Cathay: a city of 2.5 million which was a dusty border town of 10,000 people just a decade before. Now Shenzhen is where poor farm boys and girls hope to get rich quickly. So many poured into the city in the early 1990s that barbed-wire fences were erected to keep them out. But, every day, more workers move to Shenzhen at the invitation of companies who need their particular skills.

Officials estimate that the current growth rate of 30 per cent or more will continue and, by 2000, Shenzhen will have an economy nearly the size of oil-rich Alberta's. A Shenzhen municipal government spokesman said in an interview that, "by the year 2010, we will have 4.5 million people, and the same per-capita GDP as Korea and Taiwan."

This is hardly likely. But Shenzhen has been China's first experiment in capitalism, and it has been very impressive. As in America's wild west, growth has been unbelievably rapid, but unlike the wild west, where lawlessness and chaos reigned, social order has been maintained.

Bill Doo, son of a diamond merchant and son-in-law of C.Y. Tung — one of Hong Kong's wealthiest men — spoke for most Hong Kong wealthy when he said that, within five years, most of his family's sizeable assets will be in China. Doo's family owns the Ramada chain of hotels in North America, a shipping line, and real estate around the world. "In the past three years we have diversified to China because it has a fantastic future," he said.

The World Bank's chief economist in 1992 estimated that China's economy would overtake that of the United States by 2010. As for political risks, Doo said in an interview: "I've talked to some of the students who were at Tiananmen Square [during the 1989 massacre of students] and their first priority is not revolution. They want better housing or an air conditioner. Very often three generations share one room in China."

Wealth creation — not democracy — was the issue in Shenzhen, a gigantic industrial park with housing. At an intersection, loudspeakers mounted on a 60 metre billboard of Deng delivered a lecture to passers-by and motorists: "Believe in socialism, but also believe in [capitalist] reform or it is a dead end."

Some observers worried that the reform-minded Deng would be replaced by hardliners who would return to authoritarian communism. But cities like Shenzhen were not just Deng's triumph, but the Beijing bureaucracy's as well. Shenzhen was simply the first of four "special economic zones," or micro-capitalist experiments, which began in 1980, long before perestroika was even a twinkle in the Soviet Politburo's, or Mikhail Gorbachev's, eye. Besides, Beijing's reformers were further propelled toward market reforms after the former Soviet Union collapsed into untransformed chaos.

In an interview in Canada, in March 1993, Gorbachev

noted: "Thank heavens a country that big [China] is making changes. A country of 1.2 billion must take a cautious approach. In China, they are now questioning democratizing their country. The message they received from Tiananmen Square was a serious message. They will have to pursue the road of democracy. Liberalizing the economy without democratizing the society is impossible. They will not be able to make economic reforms."

Deng made the first move toward a market economy in 1978, when he gave farmers their land. Within two years, China was self-sufficient in food production. In three, it was exporting it. Then came shops, cabs, restaurants, vendors, marketplaces. By 1993, there were three more "Shenzhen" free-enterprise regions and dozens of others vying for investment and trade opportunities. The entire country was mobilized to make money.

Of course, there were potential pitfalls: China could mishandle the takeover of Hong Kong in 1997 or lose its "most-favoured nation" tariff status in the United States over the issue of human rights. The loss of that preferential tariff treatment would dampen economic activity for a while, but not permanently, as growth here is driven by manufacturers in Hong Kong, Taiwan, Korea, and Japan who simply cannot afford to operate in their high-wage countries any longer. China is destined to become Asia's, and the world's, factory.

In the absence of a relapse or showdown, China appears bent on simply creating more Shenzhens, all modelled on Hong Kong. Apart from their obvious useful economic power, they serve as useful safety valves for revolutionary-minded students. After the Tiananmen Square atrocity, it's little wonder that few are interested in democratic reforms.

As Doo pointed out, most former revolutionaries now wanted to land a job inside Shenzhen or another special economic zone where wages were 10 times higher and costs only 5 or 6 times more. All that revolutionary fervour is being harnessed by market forces. Students are not protesting or carrying placards, but most are trying desperately to get jobs with companies inside the free-enterprise zones.

Cheap labour attracted Taiwanese and Hong Kong financiers because their wages were too high. Hong Kong's manufacturing jobs dropped between 1980 and 1990 to 750,000 positions from 900,000, and have become more highly skilled along the way. Shenzhen and its province, Guangdong, saved Hong Kong's manufacturing sector from spiralling costs by allowing Hong Kong capitalists to tap into China's cheap labour pool.

By 1992, some 3 million workers in 5,000 factories in Shenzhen and Guangdong now crank out products for Taiwan and Hong Kong financiers. The accompanying land rush has reaped tens of millions of dollars in land sales and leases for Shenzhen, enabling it to build roads, sewers, and other infrastructure. All land and buildings are owned by the government.

"I think China will become a big economic power because of cheap labour," said Ming Li, managing director of Northern Telecom's Greater China region, which includes China, Taiwan, and Hong Kong. "The risk [of a political relapse] is remote, but not non-existent."

In February 1992, Northern Telecom's modern factory in Shenzhen employed 300, making PBX switching devices. Beside the plant was the workers' dormitory, and a bus to drive them to and from the city's centre for entertainment, shopping, or education jaunts. Li estimated that Northern will employ at least 3,000 workers by 1998, and will be importing huge amounts of equipment from its plants elsewhere to supply the enormous Chinese marketplace.

China's people are poor, but its government is not. Billions of dollars in foreign investment come into the country every year. By 1993, China's foreign reserves were $54.12 billion, greater than France's or Canada's. The country had few debts: China's debt is equivalent to 15 per cent of its GDP; Canada's and Italy's are 90 per cent.

In addition, China's first transformation — agrarian land reform that privatized all the farms — now spurs along industrialization. Farmers' credit cooperatives began making investments in the 1980s, and in 1992 alone invested $2.22 billion in rural industries. Prominent Hong Kong banker David Li, chairman of the Bank of East Asia, with many branches in China, estimated in 1992 that there were US$180 billion savings on deposit and another US$48 billion "under their mattresses."

SHANGHAI

The Shanghai Stock Exchange is housed in the posh ballroom of the city's first luxury hotel, built by the British in the 1800s. Digital boards flashing bid and ask prices hang between marble Corinthian columns, and rows of brokers at desks take orders over the phone. Across from the hotel is another landmark, the Seaman's Club, with its famous "Long Bar," where unwitting chaps were kidnapped and forced to go to sea. The Club dining room overlooks the wide Yangtze River and a 2-kilometre stretch of magnificent nineteenth-century European office buildings built by the various powers that partitioned the city and country. Once considered the New York City of Asia, Shanghai is the subject again of big plans in Beijing.

Fortunes have been made at this primitive, volatile stock exchange. Wealth is displayed only in certain, select night spots because this is still, technically, a communist country. Those with money worry that their wealth will be taxed, or even confiscated. But one reason that the Chinese have money is that there is so little to spend it on. Extreme buying pressure has steadily propelled stock prices upward on both Shanghai's and Shenzhen's exchanges. Interest among the members of the public is so ferocious that newly listed company shares are distributed by lottery. Last year, the first come/first served method of stock distribution in Shenzhen led to a riot. Tempers flared because policemen entrusted with the job of crowd control were allowing their friends and relatives to jump ahead of others.

China's fledgling, and relatively inconsequential, stock exchanges are going through the same growing pains that beset its burgeoning cities. But the urban area earmarked for the greatest boom is Shanghai, China's largest city, strategically located midway between the country's northernmost and southernmost coastal tips. It was sacked 1949 by Mao Zedong's communists, driving its best business brains to a then-sleepy Hong Kong. Now it is poised for greatness again should reforms continue. Already Shanghai is one of the world's 10 biggest ports and is an important gateway to China, the world's biggest potential consumer market.

One million foreign businessmen combed this city in 1992 for investment opportunities. And to facilitate business, Beijing has given Shanghai tax breaks and the freedom to sell land in order to build new highways, a subway, and massive port facilities. By 1993, city officials had about 100 representatives around the world drumming up business and investment.

"Shanghai is close to Korea, Japan, and is in the middle of our coastline," said Wang Zu-kang, head of Shanghai's Foreign Relations and Trade Commission. "In 1992 exports out of Shanghai totalled $7.86 billion in value and imports $3.84 billion. We had trade relations with 120 nations."

Unfortunately, Shanghai may also become Asia's Mexico City. The official census estimated that the population was 13 million in 1990. Unofficial guesstimates were that another 10 million people, with their worldly possessions in sacks, have poured into the city. Unlike the business visitors who inhabit Shanghai's dozens of five-star hotels, these people were crammed into residences, doorways, makeshift dormitories, or hovels made from building-site scraps and refuse. If unable to find work, some resort to crime. Others commit suicide.

Unlike new cities like Shenzhen — which has been cordoned off from the rest of the country — Shanghai has hospitals, schools, and other facilities for a permanent population in place. Housing, however, is horrid. People cram into hovels without electricity or running water. Contagious diseases of all kinds simply race through whole neighbourhoods, and squatters occupy buildings under construction or newly demolished, fashioning makeshift lean-tos out of refuse and rejected or stolen building materials.

Besides such urbanization problems, the new China must also wrestle with the problem of "social" employment or guaranteed jobs for life. Under communism, the giant state-owned companies provided workers with houses, schools, hospitals, and stores. As companies are privatized, merged, or listed on stock exchanges, they are having to adopt bottom-line concerns and lay off large numbers of people. This means government must assume responsibility from these companies for housing, hospitals, schools, and other social services, as is the case in our system. The conversion to capitalism will upset unemployed workers and may result in backlash or political unrest.

"That is why complete reforms won't happen for quite some time," explained Ji Yi-qun, deputy manager of Shanghai Port Machinery, which is gearing up to become a stock market–listed company. "This year the government gave companies permission to fire people, but companies are very cautious. This is a very sensitive issue."

He estimated that one-third of his workforce of 4,200 heavy-manufacturing workers was inefficient and unnecessary. Obviously laid-off workers will dislike reform, but those left in their jobs will be able to earn more. Both China and Russia face this daunting task of having to wean people from social luxuries that they have come to regard as entitlements.

Also left behind, of course, have been public-sector employees and pensioners on fixed incomes. As wages have risen, so has the cost of living. Like Russians who have been left to their own devices, the Chinese have been resourceful. Retirees band together to sell fast foods, and one elementary school in Shanghai sells goods in its schoolyard to supplement the teachers' paltry salaries.

HONG KONG

Driving from the airport to the island of Hong Kong can give a new arrival the wrong impression. The city's airport, surrounded by hundreds of squalid highrises, is a hazard to aeroplanes. Washing hangs out of every window on bamboo rods, giving the place a slummy, Rio de Janeiro or West Bronx feel. But, once you are through the tunnel, Asia's Manhattan suddenly appears: a vertical vision of neon and floodlights highlighting some of the world's most interesting architecture. This is like a great American city, but without the crime: everyone's too busy making money legitimately. Hong Kong is a city-state of 5.5 million people whose postage-stamp territory generates a gross national product as large as that of a handful of European countries.

It all came about by accident. Hong Kong was a backwater port controlled by Britain, then, in 1949, suddenly found itself deluged with a flood of Shanghai's best traders, financiers, and bankers. They represented most of the mainland's business brains and were fleeing from Mao Zedong's communist revolution. Shanghai expertise and British administration turned out to be a match made in heaven. Income taxes were set at a flat rate of just 17.5 per cent, and Shanghai's cunning capitalists turned the port into a manufacturing, and now financial services, powerhouse. Britain's colonial regime also created real estate fortunes by meting out land carefully, despite an exploding population. This bubble may not end in 1997, when Britain hands over Hong Kong to China, because China owns many Hong Kong buildings and wants to prop up property prices by controlling the supply of land available for development. China also has another interest. High Hong Kong property values mean the Chinese government can fetch higher prices for condos or industrial lands in Shenzhen, Shanghai, or wherever.

Hong Kong's stock market has also made many rich. For years, the Hong Kong stock market has plummeted whenever China talked tough about this city's future or whenever China's reform-minded leader, Deng Xiaoping, got the sniffles. But plenty of people suspect that China itself benefits from its pronouncements by selling short in the stock market. Popular Hong Kong legislator Emily Lau said such rumours are rampant, and suspected that they're true: "That's insider information. It's not yet a criminal offence, but it's deplorable for a government to be doing such a thing."

If mainland China is indeed playing games, that would be very naughty. But the rumours are rooted in the reality that the New China has become a cunning capitalist. In the past few years, China has embarked on market reforms that are considerably more dramatic than those underway in any of the former communist regimes in Eastern Europe, with the exception only of fast-moving Poland and Czechoslovakia.

"The IMF [International Monetary Fund] and World Bank shouldn't go to Russia to teach it the market economy. China should," cracked Yoh Kurosawa, chairman of the Industrial Bank of Japan, in a Tokyo interview.

The truth is, "Communist China" no longer exists, and when China becomes Hong Kong's landlord in June 1997 very little will happen. In fact, China, by creating four new tax havens, including Shenzhen and Shanghai, wants to create four more Hong Kongs.

Deng Xiaoping said, in a 1992 tour through southern China: "What we need is another 10 Hong Kongs." He added, "I don't know economics, but I know a good economy when I see it," when describing the rampant capitalism in his "special economic zones."

Many fretted, however, over the fact that Deng, born in

1905, was in his late eighties and that his reforms would not survive him. But no single individual could control so large a country, and China watchers guess that little will change when the old man dies. On the strength of that belief, Hong Kong investors have poured billions into China since 1988. Besides, China really does need Hong Kong: it provided Beijing with one-third of its foreign-exchange earnings in 1992. China was Hong Kong's biggest export customer. Hong Kong also provided a conduit to foreign investors and a back door for Taiwanese businessmen. Taiwan, or the Republic of China, does not diplomatically recognize the People's Republic of China.

Their dependence was mutual. China's state enterprises were Hong Kong's biggest foreign investors, with C$24 billion in real estate, cabs, Cathay Pacific Airlines, flats, Hong Kong Telecom, the Hong Kong Stock Exchange, and some 1,000 other businesses. By 1993, the mainland controlled about 30 per cent of Hong Kong's banking and insurance markets and represented virtually all the new listings on Hong Kong's stock market.

While capitalism is deeply entrenched, democracy is another matter entirely. Hong Kong was considered a test of China's commitment to capitalism and reform. Behind closed doors, in 1984, Britain and China struck a deal, called the Basic Law, for the turnover. The secret agreement extended democracy slightly by allowing for more elected Hong Kong councillors but, most important, respected contracts and private property rights and upheld the rule of law, or the independence and ultimate power of the courts over everyone, including the Beijing government itself. But since that deal, Tiananmen Square occurred and British Hong Kong governor Chris Patten tabled proposals in 1992 that called for more elected representation than had been agreed upon. China balked and talked tough. Then Washington turned up the heat by threatening to scrap China's "most-favoured nation" preferential tariff status unless it guaranteed human rights. In partial capitulation, China has been releasing dissident students who were jailed in 1989 after Tiananmen.

"I have a cynical mind and I think there was a deal between Britain and the U.S. to destabilize China's current regime, and that's not a very good idea," says Jim Abbeglen, an American management consultant and academic based in Tokyo. "Can you think of any other reason? The British haven't cared about the lack of democracy in Hong Kong for 150 years. Why, four years before surrendering it to China, do they suddenly care?"

Hong Kong legislator Emily Lau, an advocate for full democracy, pointed out another bit of British hypocrisy. "We're talking about handing over 5.5 million people here to a regime that has shown disregard for human rights," she said. "Britain went to war against Argentina to help 1,800 sheep farmers - but they were white and that war was winnable with American help. They won't even take responsibility here and give us British passports."

Lau and others demanded full autonomy for Hong Kong after the handover, or the "one country, two systems" policy China had promised. But its balkiness at the particulars of Patten's proposals caused worry that the giant would renege. That would be an economic disaster here, as people and capital would flee immediately. If China were ever destabilized, a devastating migration of Chinese people would pour into overcrowded Japan, Taiwan, Hong Kong, South Korea, and others, as has happened in Western Europe.

Hong Kong banker David Li — one of 44 advisers to Beijing on the reversion of Hong Kong's lease to China — maintained in an interview in 1992 that details will be settled amicably by 1995, two years before the official takeover. For instance, China was flexible and reform-minded and agreed quickly to U.S. demands that it sign an agreement to protect intellectual property. This concession was significant because counterfeiting of U.S. films and music costs U.S. industry billions of dollars annually. "The Chinese gave in quite easily," noted Li. "As for renewal of 'most-favoured nation' status, I would imagine the U.S. will use that as a way to stop the spread of weaponry to the Middle East."

Few people outside of the region, including U.S. congressmen, realize how dramatic China's reforms have been. Press freedoms have improved to the point where newspapers are beginning to publish scandals involving government officials if these have been exposed by the foreign press. CNN and the BBC beamed news into China's hotels. Free enterprise was rampant, the various levels of government promoting and privatizing industry in their respective regions. And, in the early 1990s, Beijing allowed lower levels of government to borrow money abroad, strike independent deals with foreigners, hand out export and import licences, and raise revenues for their own use by selling or leasing land to foreigners. Even in areas where Beijing was still in charge, its edicts were often ignored or bypassed. In other words, China had already devolved into a series of city-states and semi-autonomous provinces.

In Beijing alone, there was a waiting list of 40,000 for telephones, even though installation costs were US$700, or twice the average annual per capita GNP. By 1992, there were 10,000 portable phones in Beijing, and 2,000 satellite dishes serving hundreds of sets each. In Shanghai, a shopkeeper was fined US$5,500 by police and propaganda officials for selling satellite dishes, as were two more shops in Beijing. Even questionable modernization continues, with pawnshops, gambling, and prostitution returning.

"I think China has passed the point of no return, and after Deng dies the contest will be between personalities, not policies," commented Canada's Hong Kong high commissioner John Higginbotham, a Mandarin-speaking Chinese scholar. "I think it will be a matter of one reformer against another and business as usual in Hong Kong and China."

THE OTHER CHINA

When Shanghai capitalists were fleeing to Hong Kong, China's generals, led by Chiang Kai-shek and others, defeated by Mao Zedong's guerrilla army, crossed the China Sea in boats to Formosa. A sleepy former colony of Japan populated by ethnic Chinese, Formosa was invaded and occupied by Chiang and 2.5 million supporters. When they met resistance from the Taiwanese, they slaughtered hundreds of thousands. Chiang renamed the island Taiwan and, like Hong Kong, it settled into a benevolent dictatorship, propped up by U.S. money.

Taiwan, only 326 kilometres long, has become another economic miracle. With an economy the size of Quebec's, its 20 million people have achieved one of the world's highest living standards through hard work and large gobs of U.S. aid. But the basic underpinning for prosperity was Taiwan's fertile soil and gentle climate, which permitted the harvesting of three crops a year. Taiwan is a food exporter, a rare achievement in overpopulated Asia.

Taiwan's capital, Taipei, has a population of 3.5 million. In the early 1990s, the city is a gigantic construction site. Main thoroughfares have been ripped and boarded up for years in order to complete the subway, part of the country's ambitious $360-billion infrastructure and environment scheme.

On Valentine's Day, in 1993, the streets and stores were jammed. There were scooters and bicycles everywhere. A large department store featured shockingly expensive designer clothing, cosmetics, perfumes, and accessories. The prices were equivalent to those in Europe. So were food prices, as the Taiwanese — unable to spend money on better housing as a shortage had pushed land prices into the stratosphere - bought food and fashion instead. This day, the whole shopping area was gaudily decorated in lace and red hearts with arrows. While Valentine's Day was hardly a part of traditional Chinese culture, the event was an excuse for Chinese retailers to promote their wares.

On side streets, well-dressed families wandered through clothing shops and past ice-cream stands. On most corners, vendors sold snacks, and even whole meals. "The Taiwanese live on the streets, and most families in nice weather have their evening meal outside at one of these vendors," explained Canadian lawyer Mark Levitz, who speaks fluent Mandarin and has lived in Asia for four years.

The Taiwanese also spend lots of money on entertainment and alcohol. "KTV" clubs were everywhere, offering cut-rate drinks and karaoke singing sessions in rooms or large halls. There were also "MTV" clubs where couples could rent movies and watch them in private rooms. "They live in tiny apartments shared with grandparents, and sometimes nieces and nephews. So when young people want to get together with friends, they can't have them over. They rent a room at MTV and sit around and watch movies," said Levitz.

While life is sweet for the Taiwanese, its political leaders still have a bunker mentality because of the division of China. The government has armed itself to the teeth against the threat of a Chinese invasion. Still, Taiwan's businessmen, like Hong Kong's, have invested like mad in China. There may be two Chinas shown on maps of the world, but there is only one Chinese people. And they want to make money together, not war.

Things are gradually changing. Canada, the United States, and others now have warmer relations diplomatically with the Republic of China (Taiwan), even though we have not officially recognized its existence. (We recognize the People's Republic of China — mainland China — instead.) The partial thaw in relations may lead to a form of unification, but only if China deals amicably with Hong Kong after its acquisition in 1997.

The two Chinas demand undivided loyalty from allies and trading partners. Military trade is controversial, as France found out in 1992 when it sold $9 billion worth of jets to Taiwan. After the sale was announced, Beijing reacted immediately, unceremoniously freezing French companies out of potential contracts and ordering France to close one consulate. The French were infuriated, all the more so when China did nothing about the sale by the United States of three times as many jet fighters to Taiwan during the presidential election campaign. The mainland government merely lodged a formal protest.

Taiwan, on the other hand, reacted angrily when South Korea suddenly recognized mainland China in 1992. Taiwan unceremoniously closed its embassy in Korea and severed all ties, banning Korean imports of any kind. South Korea's switch in allegiance was undertaken because the potential China market is bigger than Taiwan's and because South Korea fears nuclear-armed North Korea and wanted the mainland as an ally.

Back in 1987, Taiwan decided to allow family reunions, then tourism, in China. Then businessmen started flocking there. Again, there is an element of schizophrenia in the conflicting policies. Taiwan does not allow direct flights or direct phone links with the mainland, but, because of the volume of travel, Taiwan's government set up an arm's-length agency — called the Strait Foundation — to deal with tourist grievances or other matters. This, their director stated emphatically, does not constitute recognition of the other China.

"Taiwan uses Hong Kong as its back door to China, and in 1992 invested C$1.4 billion and traded C$7.2 billion," estimated David Li, chairman of the Bank of East Asia. "Direct flights will come in two or three years. It's just a matter of time."

Taiwan is rich — so rich, it gave foreign aid to Russia last year. Taiwan's GDP in 1992 was the size of Quebec's, and it annually racked up trade surpluses the size of Canada's. The result was a country with little debt and $98.4 billion in foreign reserves in 1992 — the largest cache in the world and equivalent to five times Canada's foreign reserves. The Taiwanese were better off, although not yet rich. A car, for most people, was still a dream, and so was a house. But Taiwan's per-capita income jumped from $475 in 1970 to $9,015 by 1992. (Canada's was $23,800, that in the United States slightly higher.)

In mid-1993, an unprecedented meeting between Taiwan

and mainland Chinese parties took place which further reduced the risk of armed conflict between the two. As alliances form and trade grows, the region will move toward some form of freer-trade agreement, as exists in Europe and North America. Barring conflicts, Taiwan's economy — and South Korea's — may rival Canada's in size by early in the next century.

Such meteoric growth could easily be impeded; this is a part of the world which has traditionally been dogged by ugly conflicts and military conquests. Rivalries are deep and potentially violent. But rewards, flowing from economic cooperation, are becoming apparent. Already Pacific Rim nations are negotiating mini–trade deals with one another. Equally noteworthy is the fact that there are signs that Western democratic influences are catching on too. Taiwan, South Korea, and Japan are moving away from corrupt, single-party rule and becoming truly mature democracies with substantial opposition parties, vocal anti-government critics, and increasingly independent media.

THE CHINESE PEOPLE

The twenty-first century could be the Century of the Chinese People. As an ethnic group, they have been streaking ahead of the pack. As just one measure, by 1992, Singapore, Taiwan, Hong Kong, and China collectively had a staggering $200.2 billion in foreign reserves — nearly three times Japan's reserves of $70.5 billion. Of course, Japan's economy was five times the size of the "four Chinas," but arguably China's GNP was greatly understated because its official currency-exchange rate was lower than its market value. Put another way, if official GNP figures were to be believed, China's trade in 1992 was equivalent to 30 per cent of its GNP. That estimate is unrealistic: if trade were 7 per cent of its gigantic economy, China's economy would be bigger than that of the United States. Whatever the measure, the "Chinas" were catching up with double-digit growth in the 1980s, and more of the same is expected in the 1990s.

The Japanese were particularly sceptical about China's newly discovered interest in foreign investment, but have been heavily investing there anyway. Some of Japan's China experts pointed out that China had erupted into civil war every 50 years or so. Chinese responded that internal wars were often fought among Chinese warlords who were backed by opposing European powers.

"China will be destabilized as the process of modernization happens," said Professor Takashi Konami, a foreign-affairs specialist at Tokyo University. "I think China is now approaching one more big turmoil. The farmers' living standards are starting to decline. Economic changes free forces for political change, and resistance to that will create conflict."

Envy among residents in China's hinterland over the prosperity and high incomes in coastal regions like Shenzhen may result in a rift. But already power is so decentralized and flexible that the country is divided into competing camps who seem to be more preoccupied with getting ahead than with getting even.

Sony Corporation founder Akio Morita refused to join the rush by many countries into China, where low wages and liberalization has been attracting billions of dollars. "China is not safe yet," he said. "Not yet. Not for a while."

While many Japanese pooh-pooh China's prospects,

Japanese Ministry of Finance statistics tell another tale. In 1960, the United States represented 34 per cent of the world's GNP, the U.S.S.R. 15 per cent, Japan 3 per cent, and Asia 1 per cent, leaving 38 per cent for the rest. By 1989, the world's economic pie had grown, but the pieces were dramatically different in size: 22 per cent for the United States, 15 per cent for Japan, and 3 per cent for the U.S.S.R., while Asia represented 9 per cent. The ministry estimated that, by the year 2010, the Americas will represent 30 per cent, with the United States at 21 per cent; Europe will represent 40 per cent, with the European Community at 26 per cent; and Asia will have an economy the size of the Americas, or 30 per cent, with Japan at 18 per cent — nearly as large a piece as that of the United States. Interestingly, those growth projections include the possibility of an armed conflict in China, which would presumably stop economic growth and foreign investment for a period of time. Optimists feel this won't happen, and that the Asian economy will outstrip Europe's in size, and China will rival the United States and Japan in economic importance by 2010.

David Li maintains that Asia will revolve around two "triangles" — each connecting modern Asian economies with the populated hinterland of China and Siberia. "Hong Kong will be the capital of one, and Shanghai the other," he said. "Both triangles will represent the fastest-growing regions in the world for the rest of this decade. First, there is Hong Kong, Taiwan, and the Guangdong and Fujian provinces of China. This region has 120 million people, and a GDP of C$480 million already [two-thirds the size of Canada's] and will experience double-digit growth this decade. Then there's the Shanghai northern triangle, which includes Korea, northeast China, Manchuria, and the eastern provinces of the former Soviet Union."

It is possible that, as the Russian empire continues to disintegrate, the portions once belonging to China may return, voluntarily or otherwise, to the Asian fold. Manchuria and Mongolia were handed over to the Soviets by the Allies in 1945 at the Yalta Conference. Russia's invasion of Shanghai in 1858, resulted in its acquisition, in 1860, of half of northwest China and half of northeast China, now much of Siberia.

Also helping China through will be a diaspora of another 20 million prosperous ethnic Chinese living in North America, Europe, Indochina, the Philippines, and Indonesia. They are hard-working, enterprising, and committed to education and advancement for their offspring. Unfortunately, their successes have made them targets of envy in some Asian communities where their wealth is visible. In 1992, Malaysians staged a pogrom-like riot in Chinese neighbourhoods, looting shops and homes. Similar incidents have occurred throughout Asia.

China does not appear to be territorially acquisitive, despite the fact that it is overcrowded. China has 22 per cent of the world's population and only 7 per cent of its arable land. The top cop in the region, after the United States, is Russia, whose military is still amassed along the China border. Nowadays, the two, far from warring, are rapidly integrating economically. Trade is hot along the border as trainloads of Russians come to China, Mongolia, and the Koreas to buy cheap products and commodities to take home.

The Japanese have also been cozying up to the Russians, and in 1992 announced a $6-billion exploration program in Siberia. Also in that year, South Korea gave Russian president Boris Yeltsin a pledge for $3 billion worth of foreign aid over the next few years. Some felt this was no more than protection money to keep both North Korea, and possibly China, under control.

New alliances and aid are causing a shift in the region's military balance. Meanwhile, as China armed itself and Russia becomes bodyguard to South Koreans, the Americans talk about troop withdrawals there, in addition to the Philippines. Worries are that the United States will leave behind a power vacuum and more volatility, because Japan — like Germany — is the most powerful partner in its respective Triad but is frightened to re-arm or alter its constitution to allow troops to leave its borders. In both Germany and Japan, there were hand-wringing debates in 1992 over the question of deploying troops abroad. Japan eventually allowed 600 unarmed policemen to become part of the U.N. peacekeeping effort in Cambodia. But when one of the policemen was shot in May 1993, the prime minister cut his holiday abroad and jetted home to a political crisis.

Both Germany and Japan are under pressure from Americans and others who want them to pull their weight in terms of military interventions around the world.

While most Japanese opposed rearmament, Japan's Asian neighbours were buying "insurance," just in case. China spent a reported $1 billion buying armaments and airplanes from Russia. But the biggest worry in the region was North Korea's leader, Kim Il-Song — a potential Saddam Hussein. He was an isolated, nuclear hardliner in charge of a sizeable armed force, and his very existence has brought about strange alliances, such as South Korea's decision to abandon Taiwan and opt for recognition of China instead. When South Korea "bought" more protection in the form of its

$3-billion pledge to Boris Yeltsin, Russia, in turn, began charging North Korea cash for Siberian oil imports.

The point is that U.S. military hegemony has been the stabilizing factor here, and the underpinning for the incredible economic activity. That underpinning is now in question. "The U.S. is withdrawing without a doubt," says Tokyo-based consultant and professor Jim Abbeglen. "But what's the threat? China? Are they going to swim? China is not even a threat to Taiwan, which is much closer. China's deal with South Korea recognizes its right over North Korea's right to exist. China's also extended relations to Vietnam, which it is frightened of. China doesn't want trouble and it is stabilizing its borders. The real problem is that there are two big pockets of unemployed — North Korea and 160 million in China, and if they cause trouble, that's a nightmare."

The region is a paradox, said foreign-affairs expert Zbigniew Brzezinski in a speech made in Hong Kong in 1992. "This clearly is going to be the centre of gravity of global economic activity. But it is a curiously politically unstructured area when it comes to issues of global security. There may be a new Siberian or Far Eastern republic with Korea, Japan, and China. North and South China are quite different, which is a threat to unity. Why is China re-arming rapidly when the threat of the Soviets has disappeared? Is it because of a U.S. pullback and worries about Vietnam or North Korea? The U.S. has been the paramount power and created a framework in which socioeconomic change could occur stably and successfully. The American role is going to be more ambivalent. There will be some American pullback and some political tensions with China."

The Japanese are aware of this problem and have been

sounding out the possibilities of creating a regional framework to bring about political and security cooperation. But it will be difficult for Japan to pull this off in future, because of its militarism in the past. That is why Japan may lose its leadership position in the region, especially if the Chinese people make their peace politically, and the sleeping giant called China continues to emerge successfully from its socialist dark age.

JAPAN INC.

Japan is a ruthless society. Life here is about as fair and enjoyable as being in the army. In fact, Japan is a gigantic boot camp for 123 million men, women, and children. But regimentation has made Japan Inc. the most successful export nation in the history of the world. And it comes by its discipline honestly. Until 1867, Japanese military society made a living by conquering other countries. It was armed and closed to foreigners until Commodore Perry, an American, came with his black ships to Yokohama.

Japan was built on a caste system, which still exists. Only the military aristocracy, or Samurai, had surnames until the mid-nineteenth century. The rest of society was anonymous and enslaved. Samurai had the right to kill anyone without reason and without any legal consequences. Until the Second World War, rice was wealth and power. The emperor got the lion's share of the rice crop. Samurai got the next big tranche, and then the farmers. Lowest in the Japanese scheme of things were those in trade or commerce. Peasants were controlled through rice entitlements by their masters.

Japanese regimentation was most evident in their schools.

I interviewed Shunichi Takano in 1993, a teacher and a gentle man who lives three hours by train outside Tokyo. On Monday mornings, he said his grade five students were so tired that he did not bother to give them their required math lesson. Most of them attended, on top of regular school, 10 hours a week of "cram" school, and spent their only day off, Sundays, taking lessons of some kind. In 1992, Japan's education ministry granted one Saturday off per month to students in the country. Takano's school was part of a pilot project in which pupils were being given a second Saturday off per month. The ministry wanted to see if the curriculum could be covered with so much time off. "But the ministry had to ask the cram schools not to operate during that second Saturday," he said.

Children in Japan attend school 240 days a year. Teachers have no psychology or tutoring back-up and must teach classes of 40 pupils. "If I am sick or want to take a course on children with psychological problems, I have to get the principal to take my class or leave it unattended. So you really cannot take days off," Takano said.

Discipline is brutal. In early 1993, a teacher was on trial for shutting a heavy iron gate on a tardy teenager's head. The student was racing to beat the gate, and he closed it just as she entered, crushing her skull and killing her instantly. The teacher got only a one-year suspended sentence, and there was no outcry over the seeming injustice.

While brutal, Japan's schools yield results, just as its exporters do. Illiteracy is virtually non-existent in Japan. So are drop-outs. Students and their parents are driven by social pressure to succeed. In stratified Japanese society, only those who get into the best universities get the best jobs and the nicest lives. And this is not a meritocracy. Only children from wealthy families can afford the best "cram schools" or boarding schools that ensure their entry into the best universities. Not surprisingly, many of Japan's privileged and respected leaders bear one of the 10 Samurai surnames, and their children must still intermarry. By contrast, parents of retarded children often give them to orphanages; the siblings of retarded children find it impossible to marry unless the retarded children are hidden away. The pressure to excel is enormous for everyone.

"I see kids on the subway just frozen, unable to get on the car to school," said Paul Summerville, a Canadian who lives in Tokyo. "These kids have failed an examination and cannot face their friends or family with this failure. It's pathetic."

Indeed, life in the boot camp is severe, but rewarding. Inflation and unemployment are relatively low. Anyone who bought real estate before 1980 became a millionaire. The Japanese dress, travel, and eat well. In return for the 6-day work weeks and 12-hour days, companies have guaranteed their workers lifetime employment. Granted, there are signs that this system is breaking down. In late 1992, electronics giant Pioneer created a furore when it asked 35 of its 9,000 workers who were 50 years of age or older to leave as part of an early-retirement scheme. Equally shocking was the announced layoff of thousands by Nissan and JVC as a result of a collapse in profits.

While exposure to, and adoption of, Western ways eats away at the old system, abject allegiance and obedience to authority is still a given. This is why political scandals on the part of the ruling political élite are forgiven, or ignored by most. Despite free elections, only one party — the Liberal Democrats — has held power since the Second World War.

Democracy, as we know it, is non-existent.

"Japanese Westernization was rapid, an imported ideology. After the war, we built parliament and courts to convince Westerners we had a civilized way of life," explained Professor Takashi Konami. "These institutions really affect very little."

Like political Samurai, leaders in Japan have gotten away with murder. For instance, Shin Kanemaru, the Liberal Democratic Party's "kingmaker," resigned in 1992 after admitting he took $5 million from a courier firm, Sagawa Kyubin. No charges were laid. Politicians are paid paltry salaries, but allowed to accept "gifts." Also that same year, it was discovered that gangsters, members of Japan's crime organization called the Yakuza, helped Noboru Takeshita get elected as prime minister in 1987. In the fall of 1992, Takeshita denied this under questioning by opposition party members for two hours, but sordid connections were established. This scandal followed on the heels of the Recruit shares-for-favours scandal in 1989 when Takeshita's secretary committed suicide. Little wonder that a 1993 report by the Keidanren — the Japanese industrial federation — said that priorities should be political reform and a "mature democratic government."

A DAY IN YOKOHAMA

Japan's foot-soldiers live differently from Americans or Europeans. Illya Shizumi lives in Yokohama with her husband, four-year-old son, and mother, Ineko Hiyoshi. It takes her two hours and two trains to get to her six-day-a-week job at the Canadian embassy in downtown Tokyo. Her husband, an accountant, gets three or four days' holiday per year. When his company is immersed in budgets, he leaves home at 6:00 a.m. and arrives back home at 1:00 a.m. every day for weeks.

But they are lucky by Japanese standards. Their neighbourhood is posh, a mixture of mismatched houses on cramped lots, often with no more than a 90-centimetre border around the footings. Lanes are crooked, and addresses are non-existent because people rarely move. Three generations often live together. Mailmen, policemen, and neighbours know where everybody lives and what everybody does.

Illya's home is roomy. Beyond the front foyer is a tiny, paper-walled interior room, 2.7 by 2.7 metres in size, which alone was probably worth $500,000. This room was reserved exclusively for the use of Mrs. Hiyoshi, a tea master. Several times each week, she performs her tea ceremony for students in the spartan room. She explained the significance of the ritual. Special brushes, dishes, cups, flower arrangements — all symbolize a theme. When I visited, it was plum harvest time, and all her dishes bore a plum motif. Guests turn their cups to admire the design, as well they might: some of them cost thousands of dollars apiece. Kimonos cost $10,000 apiece. These are the world's most expensive cups of tea.

The cost of living is breathtaking in Japan and explains why, in part, the people work so hard: they simply must. In 1993, Illya's three-bedroom home was worth $2 million, despite a price collapse of an estimated 40 per cent, and despite its location in a separate city some two hours from downtown Tokyo. For young persons, houses are a dream. Salaries are good, but not good enough. Top-notch executives earn $100,000 a year gross, and secretaries, called "office ladies," $25,000.

Food is also exorbitantly priced. A four-course lunch without alcohol costs $120. Sushi in a hotel may be $50. Two drinks in a fancy bar with kimono-clad hostesses cost about $600. A bottle of Crown Royal costs $720.

"Cram" schools are an enormous burden on the family budget, costing $800 a month. "We should be sending him to cram school already if he wants to get into Tokyo University," said Illya about her four-year-old. "But we're not doing that. The kids are pushed too much in this country. He can be what he wants to be."

Interestingly, Japanese children are indulged and spoiled until they reach school age and become full-fledged members of the country's boot camp. As they get older, they are more and more restricted, until they end up with jobs demanding 12-hour days, 6 days a week, without holidays. This pattern is the reverse of the idealized Western upbringing where children are disciplined while young and slowly gain freedom as they get older. Not surprisingly, given the lack of room and the high cost of living, families are small in Japan, and the birthrate is below replacement levels. Demographically, Japan is the world's oldest country; by 2030, there may be one-third fewer Japanese around than there were in 1990.

Women like Illya often must survive on only four hours' sleep per night. As most wives are, she is expected to prepare a meal for her husband when he gets home from work, even if it is in the middle of the night. Ingredients, particularly seafood and vegetable staples, have to be bought fresh daily, which means that, on top of a full day's work, employed wives also have to pay a visit to a store. Illya said it was not unusual for she and her husband to sit down to dinner around midnight, then get up at 6:00 a.m. to go to work the next day.

Such a regimen should end, says Akio Morita, founder of Sony Corporation and one of Japan's most successful tycoons. Japan's single-minded pursuit of economic efficiency and success has caused tremendous trading-partner resentment. "Japanese companies should reduce their working hours," he told me in a 1993 interview. "They shouldn't let people work too long and should give more consideration for workers' lifestyles."

According to Morita's figures, Japanese workers put in an average of 2,159 hours per year; U.S. workers, 1,957 hours; German, 1,638; and French, 1,646. This has translated into another interesting difference: employee compensation as a percentage of corporate profits (an average from 1985 to 1990) is 77.3 per cent for Japanese workers; 79.9 per cent for U.S. workers; 88.2 per cent for German workers; and 86.9 per cent for French ones.

In 1992, Sony instituted for its Japanese workforce "flexible holidays" that allowed workers to take time off when they wish to rather than when the company dictates. Believe it or not, this was a big breakthrough, and upset many Japanese leaders. Sony also broke ranks by announcing that it would recruit graduates from universities other than the prestigious Tokyo University. This policy was aimed at Japan's caste system: Morita was reaching out beyond the élitist universities whose students were mostly the children of rich Samurai families.

JAPAN'S TRADE TIME BOMB

For the first time in 2,000 years of Sumo-wrestling history, the Japanese, in 1993, permitted a fat foreigner from Hawaii to become one of their Grand Champions. Another foreigner loomed within striking distance, the Tokyo newspapers announced, leading to reports that Sumo officials were formulating plans that would require all foreign Sumo recruits to be fluent in Japanese before entering the ring - a jock's non-tariff trade barrier.

Interestingly, and at long last, Japan's economy, like the Sumo ring, was also being forced open to foreign competition. Of course, as in the sports world, there are some who suspect that Japan's professed trade interest was merely a ruse, designed to fool trading partners. But Japan has a huge public-relations problem in Europe and the United States: a growing trade and current-account surplus that is already the highest in world history. Estimates are that, in 1993, Japan will earn $160 billion more than it spent or imported - a staggering surplus, equivalent to more than 20 per cent of Canada's entire economy. In 1992, Japan's surplus was also the biggest in history, ringing up $131.6 billion despite a recession at home and abroad.

Japan has the lowest level of foreign investment per person among all industrialized countries: US$180 per person, compared with US$800 in Germany, US$1,600 in the United States, and US$2,000 in Britain. Total foreign investment in Japan was US$22.8 billion by March 1992, with less than half of it from the United States. Meanwhile, Japan's total direct overseas investments were US$252 billion.

"About four-fifths of Japan's investment over the past five years was targeted at creating an economic base for growth through the 1990s," wrote Ken Courtis, an economist with Deutschebank in Tokyo. "This gives Japan tremendous momentum. Japan will emerge from the recession stronger than it has ever been because it went into the recession with the best balance sheets in two decades."

"This is the strongest economy in the world," says Dr. Jim Abbeglen, an American management consultant with Tokyo's Gemini Consulting. "But this country is really trying hard to increase imports. I've helped set up courtesy offices, but they sit empty and there are no queries. Lee Iacocca says the market is not open, but it is. Americans say this, not because they want to penetrate this market - few try - but because, by saying it, they can get protectionism back home. It's U.S. prejudice, supported by media clichés. But this is the economy that's going to control Asia, which will be the size of North America in the next century."

Others disagree, including Canadian insurance executive Terry Anderson, who has lived in Asia most of his life. "We cannot win. It's a rigged game. They say their market is open, but the Japanese send tax auditors to harass any Japanese individual who buys an American-made car. That's a non-tariff barrier. Very subtle. Very Japanese."

Japan's economy may be one of the world's strongest, and its wealth undeniable and unimpeded. But as trading partners in Europe and North America learn about some of Japan's dirty trading tricks and cope with the costs of restructuring their own economies, protectionism against Japan may increase. And the country is vulnerable because 70 per cent of its merchandise trade surplus with the United States is in vehicles alone.

Besides, like Germany or the United States, Japan will eventually have to shoulder the load in its region should its neighbours become more dangerous or erupt into conflicts or apocalyptic migrations, such as has occurred in Europe. As a result, either economic growth will slow or Japan will be out money as it assumes the financial or military obligations of keeping the local peace.

Interestingly, the Japanese fear the Chinese as much as the reverse. According to Japan's former ambassador to Canada, Michio Mizoguchi, "The Chinese are better businessmen than we are. We are wet, or emotional. They are very, very logical. China has chased us out of textiles already, some heavy industry and eventually technology. They are buying old textile and steel mills from us, then competing against us."

Of course, the rest of Asia has a great deal of catching up to do with Japan and others. The World Bank estimates that, by 2010, Europe's GDP will total US$15 trillion; the Western hemisphere's, US$11 trillion, and that of Asia, Siberia, and Oceania (which includes New Zealand and Australia, among others), US$12 trillion. It is likely that New Zealand and Australia, both Anglo Saxon countries, will cast their economic lot with North America through its free-trade agreement, for cultural and other reasons.

But such GDP figures are totally misleading and understate the true size of developing countries with unreliable currencies such as China. In 1993, the International Monetary Fund addressed this problem and dramatically revised the measurement, basing it on purchasing-power parities, which take into account international difference in prices. Previously, the IMF would add up a country's output in its own currency, then convert that into dollars at market-exchange rates.

This method tripled China's share of world output, making it the world's third-biggest economy, behind the United States with 22.5 per cent and Japan with 7.6 per cent. Under the old method, China's GDP in 1992 was only US$440 billion, or US $370 per head. "That is an economy smaller than Canada's," *The Economist* stated, "and an income per head only slightly higher than India's — hard to square with China's high life expectancy and daily food consumption, not to mention household ownership of consumer durables. (Nearly 70 per cent of Chinese urban households now have colour televisions and 81 per cent have washing machines.)"

By this measure, China will easily overtake Japan as Asia's largest economy in the twenty-first century.

ASIA'S TIGERS

Asia's prosperity will hinge, in great measure, upon the success of China's leaders in bringing about reforms without creating chaos within their country. Internal problems in China could lead to civil war, border disputes, and mass migration into neighbouring economies. But if China transforms itself into the world's biggest cheap-labour factory without incident, it will simultaneously become the world's biggest consumer market. This will provide unique new opportunities to high-cost Japan, South Korea, Taiwan, Hong Kong, and Singapore, who will increasingly be pestered by Western protectionism.

Interestingly, East Asia's ascendancy will provide other Pacific Rim nations, such as the United States, Canada, Australia, and New Zealand, with newfound opportunities. With huge land masses and resources, these four are destined in the next century to become Asia's breadbaskets and raw-materials suppliers. Other opportunities will include the supply of technology and infrastructure development for power generation, housing, transportation, health care, and telecommunications.

Asia's rapid economic development, and the dismantling of the Soviet Union, could also bring about new trading relationships between the former Soviet republics in Central Asia as well as with the Asian portion of the Republic of Russia, or Siberia. Already trainloads of traders and goods have created a modern version of the Silk Road, linking East with West.

Unfortunately, Asia is a potential tinderbox of armed conflicts over everything from religion to land and political beliefs. A flare-up is made more than possible because of the security and moral vacuum in the region, apart from the presence of the United States. But the Americans will gradually withdraw, as they have from Europe, even though there is nothing to take their place, apart from U.N. peacekeepers. That will have to do, even though the force is overstretched and inadequate, as events in Yugoslavia have proved. The logical choice for leader is economically pre-eminent Japan. But the Japanese people are unwilling to assume this role because of their unfortunate militaristic past of violence and tragedy. That possibility frightens many in Asia too, particularly the Chinese, who suffered the most as a result of Japanese aggression. While understandable, the power vacuum makes the region vulnerable, and inaction, as Europe demonstrated with regard to Yugoslavia, merely results in disruption, mass migration, and economic chaos.

THE
OUTCASTS

RUSSIA

ANY COUNTRIES IN ASIA ARE GETTING THEIR economic acts together and have entered the category of up-and-comers known as developing countries. Malaysia, Thailand, Indonesia, China, India, and others have created prosperous middle classes as a result of market reforms, good educational systems, and sheer hard work. They will eventually form a gigantic Asian trading bloc. Similarly, Latin America is beginning to improve slowly and will, no doubt, be helped by the United States through membership in a Western-hemispheric trade zone. Australia and New Zealand will likely opt to join North America's trading bloc, preferring to be partners with "Anglo Saxon" countries like the United States and Canada, rather than be alone or be gobbled up economically by Asia. Then there is Western Europe, postponing a merger with its six neighbouring Eastern-bloc nations, but destined to form one.

Such realignments will, in the long run, benefit the countries involved. But they will also create orphan nations. Shunned by the developing triad in North America, Europe, and East Asia are the new countries that were formerly part of the Soviet Union as well as nations in Africa and the Middle East. The Soviets have a head start, but it still may take a generation or more for the Russians and others to get the hang of capitalism. At least they have roads; bridges; schools; housing; and a talented, educated populace. All they need are enlightened leaders and a change of culture to foster hard work and initiative. By contrast, Africa and the Middle East are going to be in worse shape in the next century than they are in this one unless drastic, and fundamental, changes occur.

By the end of the century, a few dozen new countries will probably form as borders shift or are captured. Russia itself will continue to fall apart, and is already, in my opinion, a figment of the imagination. Is Russia still a country when, in 1993, eight of its republics had unilaterally declared independence? Or when a handful more refused to sign the Russian confederation treaty and were passing their own reforms in contravention of Moscow's? And when others were diverting revenue away from Moscow and into their own coffers? The reality is that Russia, with its 11 time zones and dozens of ethnic groups, cannot remain one country unless Moscow can bribe the republics to stay within its confederation or force them to through armed intervention. Virtually bankrupt, Moscow cannot afford to do either. So, the country may continue to divide.

As Russia remains preoccupied with its own struggles, the six Eastern-bloc countries have turned toward the reluctant West for trade and aid. The three Baltic republics — Estonia, Latvia, and Lithuania — are busy building relationships with the old Hanseatic alliance of Scandinavian countries. Ukraine remains frozen at the reform switch, preoccupied with internal problems and a fear of Russia. The six Central Asian republics also aim to wean themselves from Moscow, but remain immersed in economic and land-claim problems.

Siberia is an unknown, and may eventually leave Russia. One of the largest, and richest, Russian republics in Siberia has already declared independence and has been busily forming alliances and doing trade deals with the Chinese, Koreans, and even the Japanese. Its future uncertain, Russia remains in chaos, with little hope of meaningful reform because leaders are divided between reformers and old communist hardliners who don't want changes to be made. But the people have come out of their capitalistic closets and are trying to survive. Some are doing exceptionally well. But, rich or poor, most suffer from the stress of adaptation in a country that's been turned upside down.

SURVIVAL, SOVIET STYLE

The cosmonaut Sergei Krikalyov was stranded in space for 10 months. He was just weeks away from running out of food and oxygen when the German government spent $28 million to launch a spacecraft manned by a German test pilot and plucked the cosmonaut out of space. When Krikalyov left earth on May 19, 1992, his country was the Soviet Union, his home town was Leningrad, his president was Mikhail Gorbachev, and the hammer-and-sickle flew over the Republic of Kazakhstan. When he arrived back on March 25, 1993, his country had disappeared, his home town was called St. Petersburg (as it had been before the communist revolution), Gorbachev was a private citizen, and Kazakhstan was a sovereign nation.

Moscow's once-great space program was in tatters. So was just about everything else. But that was hardly surprising. The biggest factor contributing to the collapse of communism was the fact that the Soviet Union had gone bust. It had taken Washington 40 years and US$5 trillion to push the Evil Empire into the equivalent of Chapter 11 bankruptcy. And, left in its place, were 15 bankrupt republics lurching from crisis to crisis. Unlike other bankruptcies, unfortunately, the same incompetent managers who caused the collapse remained in charge in the aftermath. Not surprisingly, only a handful had viable business plans to turn matters around, and few had changed the locks on the door. The result was that assets were disappearing into the hands of unscrupulous leaders and their foreign accomplices.

The result is near anarchy as individual Russians, Ukrainians, and others have resorted to everything from the abandonment of their trained circus animals to the purloining of equipment or assets in order to survive. Few considered such acts to be theft because the state owned everything and, once the state fell apart, there was no one to protect the state's interests. Goods left factories, only to be pilfered by truck drivers, crooked store employees, or thieving strangers before they could reach store shelves. Party bosses in charge of companies took bribes or cut personal deals with foreigners, selling them everything from tanks to real estate. Sometimes foreigners bought from people who were not entitled to sell. The Russian sellers made off with the money, and their buyers ended up owning nothing.

"The business publication *Commersant* was sold to the *Wall Street Journal* recently," said Artyom Borovic, editor–in–chief of *Top Secret*, a twice–monthly tabloid with a circulation of 3.5 million readers. "Then the publication was sold again, out from under the *Journal*, to a French tycoon who now owns it."

There's a joke which describes business, Russian style, said Jeff Barrie, an American businessman living in Moscow: "One guy says, 'I want $10,000 for a tonne of butter,'and the other guy says, 'I'll give you $8,000.' They shake hands. Then one guy goes out to find $8,000 and the other goes out to find a tonne of butter. Nobody really owns anything. That's Russian business."

The heists were huge. Foreign bank accounts were illegal without government permission, and yet billions were spirited out of the country by unknown individuals. Policemen, their livelihood ravaged by the collapse of the ruble, shook down motorists on the streets of Moscow.

The week I was in Kiev, Ukraine, in February 1992, the entire country ran out of gasoline. Cabs, buses, and factories came to a standstill for seven days. Why? Because production from its two refineries was diverted for export to a mysterious Canadian company. The next announcement I heard was to the effect that several Ukrainian submarines would be sold from its Black Sea fleet to Iran, an unquestionably dangerous country. Both announcements embarrassed the government.

The truth was that the Ukraine's fledgling government signed over many of its state-owned enterprises on long-term leases to managers drawn from the old Communist Party ranks. These leases, still in effect, allowed these men to run their companies as though they owned them. Not surprisingly, many got spectacularly rich by pocketing some of the proceeds of selling patents, signing export contracts, or transferring technology to the highest bidders. The gasoline fiasco eventually brought home to the public the foolishness of this practice, and a probe discovered what had happened. The head of the oil monopoly and the shipping company personally pocketed millions for selling assets the public owned. Both men were fired in late 1992. The energy minister was also removed from his job.

Most bizarre was the outcome of my attempt to go to Chernobyl, site of the world's worst known nuclear accident. Many had died, and thousands had suffered the long-term effects of radiation sickness after a fire had swept through the facility in 1986. A ministry official agreed that I could go. Two days later, when I called to confirm the excursion, the trip was called off because, said the official, the "rights" to an area around Chernobyl some 30 kilometres in radius were "owned" by a California outfit called Multi Entertainment Holdings Inc. Permission had to be obtained, and a fee paid, but no one knew how to get in touch with the California outfit. Eventually, I tracked down the company in Sherman Oaks, California, and interviewed a principal, Tim Davis, who claimed that the rights for an indefinite period of time were bought from a Moscow government agency. Multi Entertainment was a family business that had done deals with Russians for years. "We decided to get the zone rights to Chernobyl because it just appealed to us at the time," said Davis.

Then I was tipped off that opium poppies were being grown in the acreage surrounding Chernobyl. This allegation was denied by Ukraine, but it was obvious that such a protected, contaminated area would be the perfect camouflage for heroin refining and transshipment. In early 1993, the U.S. Customs Department issued a report stating that hundreds of millions of dollars' worth of heroin was intercepted and confiscated in Eastern Europe from Eastern European sources. Several of the Central Asian republics, formerly part of the Soviet empire, had legalized poppy growing.

In 1992, Moscow admitted that US$32-billion worth of gold bullion was missing, and New York's crack private eyes, Kroll and Associates, were being hired to track down the missing treasure. Another US$12 billion disappeared from banks in the former Yugoslavia. It was widely suspected that corrupt communist officials had the gold and cash smuggled to Latin America, where the bullion was swapped for cash with drug cartels eager to launder their ill-gotten gains. Russia's missing gold was security for foreign banks who lent the dying regime of Mikhail Gorbachev US$62 billion. It's unlikely that lenders will ever be repaid: the money was owed by the Soviet Union and, since January 1, 1992, there has been no Soviet Union.

Mikhail Gorbachev questioned the figures bandied about concerning missing funds and assets in an interview in March 1993. "What is indeed a fact is that foreign trade liberalization let companies trade freely and there has been some capital flight of money not returned to Russia. I believe that's very bad because what we need is precisely this money. There's about US$75 billion in Western bank accounts because people are not sure if they should return it to Russia because they won't be able to use it to buy necessary equipment and pursue modernization. The foreign exchange policy also provides no incentive to bring money back to Russia. This is an important issue."

Gorbachev continued: "The economic situation is unstable, and Russian businessmen think things may turn out badly. Some think forces might win which won't let government institutions be stable."

"I'm frightened. People are stealing everything because the country's falling apart," said Geoffrey Carr-Harris, a successful Canadian businessman in Moscow. Owner of the Alpha Graphics franchise in Moscow, with two locations, he was badly shaken the day I arrived for an interview. A woman friend had been murdered the day before, shot after handing robbers her wallet and purse.

"They need a psychiatrist on every street corner," he explained. "These people exhibit all the symptoms of abused children. They were lied to and punished for nothing, brutalized and living under huge restrictions. As a result, they do not trust, they are not trustworthy themselves, and they have low self-esteem. Getting good workers is a huge, huge problem."

People are desperate. By 1993, the country was on the verge of economic anarchy — or hyperinflation of nearly 50 per cent a month. The ruble was turned into rubble as the incompetent communists still in government simply cranked up the printing presses to pay salaries or to buy votes. Average monthly salaries were the equivalent of $10 per month. People on fixed incomes were surviving on potatoes and bread. Prices for gas for taxicabs and private vehicles had skyrocketed, and shortages were commonplace as black-marketers hijacked government supplies and sold them for hard currency. Whole regions were without heat and light. Refugees from war-torn areas were arriving in the thousands. Crime had increased everywhere. Army weapons generally went missing, sold to the highest bidder. Many feel that the well-armed Serbians have been waging war with weapons sold to them by Russian military officials.

New Russian millionaires like Constantine Borovoy employed 15 bodyguards to protect himself and his family from kidnappers and extortionists. A former math professor who had made his fortune launching the Russian Commodities and Raw Materials Exchange in Moscow, Borovoy was pessimistic when I spoke to him. He was convinced that the bad old days of communism would recur in the absence of a government that knew what it was doing. "I think there will eventually be a war with Ukraine over Crimea, and a fascist coup with military backing," he said.

The federal government had become irrelevant as Boris Yeltsin and his Congress of Deputies debated endlessly over reforms. Local governments were taking matters into their own hands in the absence of policy direction. For instance, Russia's third-largest city, Nizhni Novgorod, had already embarked upon a transformation of the economy to free enterprise by privatizing shops, raising money through the sale of municipal bonds, and investing the proceeds. The city fathers also privatized farms, setting up Russia's first local land banks where farmers could borrow money, using their land as collateral. City fathers also diverted from Moscow half the profits and taxes paid by local defence firms and put the money into a conversion bank which was investing in firms that converted from military production to consumer products. Although most of these schemes were technically illegal, the city was simply proceeding with its own reforms.

THE TYRANNY OF AVOSKA

Everywhere along the streets of Soviet cities, pedestrians carried string-bags called "avoskas," which, in Russian, means "by chance." These bags were essential because stores, and shoppers, never knew in advance what would be in stock on government store shelves. With *avoskas*, people would load up with extras, in essence forward-buying whatever they came across "by chance." They would buy pickles when they really needed milk and butter, but would barter the pickles with neighbours or on street corners for cash or goods they really wanted. This lack of distribution based on consumer need or desire led to hoarding, which, in turn, created even more shortages. People were forced to load up with whatever was available for barter. Others were "arbi-traging," or paying government prices at one location and reselling for the market price elsewhere. During the weeks I was in Moscow, one high-rise balcony broke from its moorings and plunged 12 storeys to the ground, narrowly missing pedestrians. It had been overloaded with bags of hoarded refined sugar.

Wealthy Russians or foreigners had begun to hire full-time "shoppers" rather than pay the obscene prices for food and other groceries at the spiffy new "hard currency stores" licensed by the government. These stores were charging higher–than–Western prices for items because of their captive market. The dual system made life miserable. Personal administration — such as shopping, or even buying rail tickets — ate up two or three hours per day. There were no home deliveries, special orders, or even telephone directories to look up specialty shops. Consumers looking for specific items would spend hours trying to find a shop containing them, then line up for hours more inside the shop, waiting for someone to fetch it; then wait some more for someone else to take their money.

Despite such hardship, people were incredibly ingenious. Hordes of wholesale entrepreneurs formed gigantic sidewalk sales throughout Moscow. These spontaneously sprang up in public in early 1992 after Yeltsin issued a decree ending government monopolies and allowing individuals to buy and sell. In the old days, individuals who broke the law were pursued by the KGB and punished severely as "black-marketeers" or "speculators."

Ironically, on February 27, the biggest sidewalk sale in the city was near the hated KGB headquarters, with its underground cells. The gathering of 5,000 or so vendors was a primitive version of the first rule of retail success — location, location, location. The site was high-traffic - around the corner from the Metropole Hotel near the Kremlin, the ballet house, and many office complexes. Even better, prospective customers streamed out of a nearby subway entrance, and the backdrop to all the activity was the city's largest children's department store.

The sidewalk, 9 metres wide, was impassable. In the slush and the snow and the grime, the entrepreneurs formed a series of lengthy gauntlets for shoppers to push their way through. Queues of sellers faced inward, holding up shampoo, shoes, jams, vodka, Barbie dolls, clothing, and even camera equipment. In essence, these people were two-legged retail outlets.

With the aid of a translator, I interviewed a young man on the edge of the throng. He was holding a bright red suitcase, and both he and a friend were smiling, despite the dismal weather and the crush. His name was Vladislav. He was a 23-year-old hairdresser from Samara, 24 hours by train from Moscow. He was selling his suitcase. "The only suitcase factory in Russia is in my town," he explained. "I paid 120 rubles for this suitcase, and it is worth 600 rubles here. I will be happy to get 400 rubles or so, which will cover my expenses and give me enough to get home and to buy hair-spray, which is not available in my city of Samara because the only hairspray factory is in Moscow."

Vladislav was taking advantage of the fact that Russia had not raised public transportation prices to reflect anything near the value of the service, salaries, or fuel. The communist system gave no credit for the cost of capital and never kept books, as capitalists do. So, for example, it cost just 0.0007 cents to ride on Moscow's enormously expensive, and excellent, subway system — sunk four storeys below ground because it was also a nuclear-proof air-raid shelter. A two-hour flight from Moscow to Kazan, near the Ural Mountains, cost only $1.68 one way, and a trip across the 11 time zones of Russia via the Siberian rail system cost $5.00.

This insanity was perpetuated because fuel had no value in Soviet Russia because it was produced, refined, and distributed by the government. The people employed in the oil industry could not survive on their minuscule and depreciating ruble salaries, so there was theft, black-marketeering, and absenteeism. Simultaneously, the suppliers to the oil and refining industries were going broke or shutting down, with the result that everything from steel for pipelines to wrenches for repairs was unavailable.

For instance, the government's monopoly airline, Aeroflot, paid US$3 a tonne for domestically refined jet fuel worth US$300 per tonne. The refiners, in turn, paid only US$0.09 per barrel to the oil-producing provinces to buy crude oil worth US$19 a barrel.

The same silliness was apparent in other "prices." It was not uncommon, for instance, for central planners to divert bread from bakeries to farms for use as cattle feed, if there was a shortage of regular feed. The rationale was that bread baked by Russians was "free," whereas grain was "valuable," particularly if bought with hard currency from foreign countries like Canada or the United States.

After the collapse of communism, authority had broken down and hyperinflation had destroyed buying power. So cash-starved industries began to "divert" their production to the black market or for export. Doing so was easy for refineries and oil-producing provinces, and the hard-currency earnings undoubtedly ended up mostly in the Swiss bank accounts of the bureaucrats who signed the export licences. But sometimes the money was used to keep the system running.

No matter who profited from them, these diversions caused even more shortages. For instance, a British geologist living in Russia told me that foreigners flying Aeroflot were routinely shaken down for hard currency by crew members just before departure to bribe ground crews in order to get fuel. One plane crashed, killing everyone on board, because the pilot was short-changed on fuel by greedy ground crews and it went undetected because the plane's fuel gauges were broken.

What was most amazing, in early 1992, was how Russians with scruples were somehow able to profit legitimately from this economic madness. Like Vladislav travelling by train with his suitcase, hundreds of individuals were trading madly with the People's Republic of China, North Korea, and the Indian subcontinent. They would load up with food or consumer products, then transport their wares back to Russia's more prosperous population centres. On every trainload, said a businessmen I interviewed, there were scores of products piled shoulder high on empty passenger seats purchased by such entrepreneurs. Some even used camels or horses, as in days of old, to bring back goods from Asia to Europe along the ancient Spice Road.

But life was hardship or hustle in the absence of a viable system or currency with purchasing power. At the same sidewalk sale where Vladislav shivered, two tough-looking Ukrainians were perched with cases of vodka at the mouth of the subway entrance. Looking like Central Casting's version of gangsters, they maintained that they were teachers from Ukraine. Vodka, they explained, was rationed in Ukraine — two bottles per adult per month — and they bought undesired rations from teetotallers for 40 rubles a bottle. Their price in Moscow was 80 rubles a bottle. It was more likely, I concluded, that their vodka had come from an illegal still or had been stolen from the government distillery or liquor store with assistance from its employees.

Inside the children's department store, the scene was surprisingly similar to that in the street market. Vendors holding up their goods lined the aisles of the store, blocking from view the store's shelves and counters. A young woman named Lena, who described herself as an "economist" and spoke excellent English, was holding up for sale a child's sweater in front of a sweater counter.

"Don't they ask you to leave?" I asked.

"They say over the loudspeaker that we should leave, but we all ignore the message," she says.

And nothing happened, because nobody "owned" the store except the state. The people in charge of the store were getting paid whether or not anything was bought, so they really didn't care about vendors "trespassing."

Lena was on her lunch hour — even though it was 11:00 a.m. She said a colleague was covering for her at her place of employment. Tomorrow, she said, she would go to work

140

and cover for her colleague. "I'm selling this sweater because it was a present for my daughter and is too small," she explained.

In the West, a consumer would simply take the item back to the store to exchange it for the correct size, but that was impossible here. Soviet stores never ordered inventory, but merely stocked whatever the state-owned factories produced and shipped to them. Consumers could not phone around to find someone with the correct size because there were no telephone directories. Store clerks were no help because they had no idea what would arrive next. The only option was to swap or sell the item and buy something completely different or pocket the profits.

I also stopped an elderly woman who was holding five rolls of pastel wallpaper. I asked her what she thought about this gigantic sidewalk sale. "It's a mess," she said. "Look at this, look at what the government has done. This is just a horrible mess. But I'm happy with my wallpaper even though I came here to buy shoes."

Pensioners on fixed incomes were the obvious victims of hyperinflation and economic anarchy. Many "babushkas" were forced to farm themselves out as professional "shoppers," willing to search, and then line up, for hours. Less enterprising or energetic seniors merely performed that function for their sons and daughters with whom they lived.

DESCRAMBLING THE EGG

The division of the Soviet Union into 15 republics destroyed their economies overnight because of the way the empire's industries were organized. Josef Stalin created gigantic factory monopolies. Bulgaria, for instance, was the location for the only forklift-truck manufacturer in the former Soviet Union and Eastern bloc. Hungary was where the region's only bus manufacturer was located; East Germany, its railway sleeper-car maker; and so on. Wheels needed for assembly in Hungary's bus plant were not available from the wheel factory because it was located in a newly independent, and perhaps hostile, former Soviet satellite. Worse yet, parts were often not available because of wars or bankruptcy.

For example, 2,000 unfinished engines littered the Hammer and Sickle Diesel Engine Factory in Ukraine. They were unfinished because the company's customer — a Russian combine-tractor plant — could not pay for the Ukrainian engines, its only source of supply. Without a customer, Hammer and Sickle could not finish the engines. The Russian factory could not finish its tractors and combines because its customers, collective farmers, had not paid their debts. The farmers, in turn, were obliged to sell their produce and products to state-owned stores and food-processing factories that paid them in rubles, which depreciated hourly due to an inflation rate of 50 per cent per month.

Fused in deadly economic union, the dismantled Soviet Union fell apart economically. Inter-republican trade virtually disappeared, slicing 20 per cent or more off everyone's economic activity. Ukraine, for instance, obtained 70 per cent of its imports from Russia and sold 30 per cent of its exports to Russia. This two-way trade, except for oil and natural-gas sales, ceased because Ukraine was broke and was using an interim currency which consists merely of a "coupon" that the Russians could not use in their economy. They could not cash in coupons because there was neither a banking system nor currency exchange.

In the absence of a trade infrastructure, the former Soviet Union was nothing more than a series of industrial white elephants producing military goods or consumer products, almost all of which were unsaleable in the West. Workers and managements were trying to improvise and find new markets, but most were hopeless because they had no idea about the market economy. Sadly, one enterprising airplane factory management team thought it would get around the export ban on kevlar (a rare light-weight material) by selling kevlar miniature planes. Ignorant of prices, the miniature planes were sold to Westerners who paid less for them than the kevlar itself was worth on world markets. These foreign traders bought the miniatures then sold them immediately for their raw-material value and made huge profits.

Equally troublesome, and potentially dangerous, was trying to descramble Stalin's "Russification" process, which involved a form of colonization of the Soviet Union. Regionally and ethnically disparate, the empire was made more cohesive and controllable by transplanting millions of ethnic Russians into the outer regions of the vast territory. At the same time, a policy of relocating Ukrainians, Georgians, and various other minorities into other regions was undertaken. The result was that, by 1992, some 25 million Russian ethnics lived in the now-independent republics — vulnerable, isolated, and potential victims of "ethnic cleansing." A total of 75 million former Soviet citizens were living outside their ethnic groups' natural boundaries. In the Baltic states, for instance, ethnic Russians were denied the vote by an edict in 1992, even though they comprised as much as 40 per cent of the population of Lithuania, Latvia, and Estonia. In retaliation, Russia punished the Baltic republics by selling oil and natural gas to them at world prices and payable only in hard currency. The result was rationing, blackouts, and economic hardship.

Lacking coherent economic policies, Russia and its neighbours were in danger of sinking. They have been unable to undertake needed agrarian land reform even though evidence of results was available. Not only had the People's Republic of China handed over its land to farmers in 1978 and become self-sufficient in food within two years, but 3 per cent of Russian farmland had been privatized and provided 25 per cent of the country's agricultural output. Bickering among politicians prevented reforms.

"[Russian president Boris] Yeltsin is both a democrat and a communist. He made a U-turn six years ago and he can make a U-turn again," commented one of Moscow's most well-known political journalists, Artyom Borovic. "As we say 'the mummy [Lenin's tomb] is still in the square' and that has a mystical power. This is a country which hates rich and successful people and may never embrace capitalism."

Everyone I interviewed was pessimistic. The best guess among most was that a charismatic "brown," or nationalist with military backing, would take over the country eventually. These fascist elements wear brown shirts, as did Hitler's Nazis. Until that happened, the military was keeping itself busy as a peacekeeping force, but on a selective basis. Yeltsin "collected" $3 billion in foreign aid from South Korea, which is concerned about Russia's former ally, North Korea. Yeltsin deployed peacekeepers in Moldavia and South Ossetia, part of Georgia and Azerbaijan, to protect Russian minorities. But when summoned to help out in Armenia, where few Russian ethnics live, Moscow refused. Some republics claim that Moscow is using its peacekeeping efforts to pursue its own interests.

The biggest concern has been that unauthorized parties would get possession of some of the Soviet's 31,000 tactical nuclear weapons. In early 1990, Azerbaijani rebels nearly captured nuclear weapons stockpiled in Azerbaijan. Unless carefully guarded, nuclear devices could be obtained by terrorists, Islamic fundamentalists, or other fanatics.

THE MATRIOSHKA

Street vendors set up shop everywhere in Russia, and one of the most popular souvenirs is a political version of the nest of *matrioshka* dolls within dolls within dolls. These cup-shaped dolls are hand-painted caricatures of former Soviet leaders, beginning with a hand-sized Yeltsin doll tapering down to a Gorbachev, Brezhnev, Khrushchev, Stalin, and finally a Lenin doll the size of a pinkie finger. The Soviet Union got smaller and smaller, like a *matrioshka*, until it disappeared altogether. The same happened to Yugoslavia, the Republic of Russia, and perhaps even China, although reformers have kept that giant glued together by providing new prosperity and by force, such as the army violence in Tiananmen Square in 1989.

But the Tatar flag flapped above the white-washed castle in Kazan, Tatarstan. Its president, in an interview in February 1992, made no bones about his intention to lead his province out of the Russian federation to independence. Just one month later, on March 21, 1992, Tatarstan residents would vote in a referendum for independence. Its leaders are among the many Russian republics that have refused to sign Russia's confederation treaty. Tatarstan and Bashkortostan are among the many Moslem portions of

Russia that are drifting toward independence and an alliance with their sovereign neighbours to the south, the six Central Asian republics that broke away from the Soviet Union. "We want a new treaty with Russia to enable us to realize our economic potential. We want Russia to delegate powers to ourselves without violating the integrity of Russia," said Tatar president Mintimier Shaimiev. Of course, if all of Russia's 31 provinces refused to sign the constitution and declared independence, as Tatarstan has done, there would be no Russia any longer — only a gigantic military force without a tax base to support it. Of course, each of the 15 republics now has its own army or militia.

Both Kazan and Ufa Bashkortostan are cities that lack skylines, except for the mosques. Government buildings flew their own flag and had declared as official languages Tatar and Bashkiri, which are Turkish tongues. Tatarstan had been an important outpost during the years of the silk trade between ancient China and medieval Europe, and the cities more recently are located at a strategic crossroads of rail links with Siberia and oil pipelines. About the size of Nova Scotia, Tatarstan produced 240 million barrels of oil a year, equivalent to Ecuador's or Alberta's production. Bashkortostan was equally resource rich.

To a Westerner, the most striking thing about Shaimiev and his Bashkiri counterpart, President Murtaza Rahimov, was that they were decidedly more Oriental in appearance than Occidental. That brought home the reality that Russia was really the last of the great empires. With dozens of ethnic groups still within its boundaries, the centre could not hold. How could privileged white Europeans in Moscow control a hinterland 11 time zones wide, populated mostly by Muslims and Chinese?

A trip to these two provinces — some 800 kilometres southeast of Moscow — revealed how much ethnic nationalism had risen. Provincial names had been changed to Tatarstan, from the Russian Tataria, and Bashkortostan, from Bashkiria, to reflect Asian and Moslem roots. Mosques were springing up everywhere, built by Islamic fundamentalists from Iran who pushed for a Tatar-Moslem "homeland."

It was estimated that throughout Russia there were 1.2 million Bashkiris and 7 million Tatars, with nearly half living in these two wealthy Russian provinces. One of Russia's most respected analysts, Georgy Arbatov who heads the Institute for U.S. and Canada, a Moscow think tank, is convinced that Russia's other provinces (called "autonomous republics") won't leave, but agrees that Tatars represent a special case, like Ukrainians. Attempts to Russify their cultures failed abysmally, despite seven decades of trying.

"Most 'republics' still within Russia have large Russian populations, averaging 50 per cent. But the Tatars are the exception and have something - a statehood," commented Arbatov in an interview in Moscow.

Their languages are a derivation from Turkish, even though they themselves are descendants of Genghis Khan's nomadic forces. A conference held in spring 1992 in Turkey launched an informal Pan-Turkish arrangement with former Soviet republics, many of which were part of the Ottoman Empire for centuries. The Central Asian republics of Kyrghyzstan, Kazakhstan, Tajikistan and portions of others are also populated by Moslems.

THE OIL MYTH

The conventional wisdom, before the Soviet collapse, was that Russia would fare the best among all Central and Eastern European countries in making the transition to a market economy because of its enormous resource wealth. But the resource industry is a nightmare of incompetence, environmental problems, and corruption.

Usinsk, one hour's drive from the Arctic Circle, in the province of Komi, is a drab Soviet town of 40,000, surrounded by some of the richest oil fields in Russia. The town was a series of treeless neighbourhoods of grey, peeling highrise towers.

In February 1992, crammed into makeshift offices which once housed the Communist Party, were two dozen Canadians employed by Gulf Canada Ltd., which was involved in a joint venture with the province's oil company. In essence, they were there to help Russia capitalize on its enormous oil wealth. But Russia wasn't making it easy.

Western investment and technology are badly needed. Gulf signed a deal in 1991 with the Russians and with its partner, British Gas PLC, pledged to provide up to US$280-million worth of management and technical help. In return, the Russians would provide workers, export permits, and a field with an estimated 800 million barrels of oil situated conveniently near oil pipelines. But conditions were primitive, and merging two different oil cultures was difficult.

"I was in the Beaufort Sea with Gulf, but at least in Tuktoyaktuk we had telephones and airports that worked," says Gulf logistics coordinator Jim Guthrie. "This is awful."

For instance, Gulf officials were unable to reach their Moscow head office using local telephone links, so they installed an expensive satellite phone line — costing $30 a minute to use — to call Calgary, which, in turn, relayed information to Moscow.

Life for locals is horrid. There's no such thing as a block heater; motorists light fires under their engines in the morning to get their vehicles started. Trucks are started with hand cranks. Business is hard to conduct because there are no cellular phones, no couriers. Hotels have no hot water, toilet paper, or bathtubs. Guests shower in communal bathrooms, one bathroom per 20 rooms. Office supplies — from paper clips to toilet paper — have to be flown in from Calgary.

The bureaucratic obstacles were awful too. The joint venture concept was that Gulf, using Western techniques, would coax more oil out of existing oilfields. The Russians had no idea how to do secondary or tertiary recovery and were able to get only 10 per cent of a reservoir. Gulf, like other Western outfits, routinely recovered 27 per cent of a reservoir. By August 1992, Gulf was producing some 15,000 barrels a day out of the field and had exported 2 million barrels to Germany. Then business, Russian style, took over. "Moscow reinterpreted the agreements and we stopped exporting in August while this was being decided," said Gulf spokesman John Sparks. "But the impediments are not deal breakers, and we're confident we'll resolve it."

Changing the rules midstream added insult to injury. Foreign sales were conducted through a government monopoly which paid a single averaged-down price for oil whether it was top-quality crude worth US$19 a barrel or low-quality crude worth US$12 a barrel. Besides, the monopoly paid for only 90 per cent of the oil put in the pipeline because only 90 per cent came out the other end. The rest leaked into the environment. The ecological damage was horrendous, and Russia's 37,000 kilometres of oil pipelines were often submerged in self-created oil lakes.

Gulf resolved the dispute in early 1993, and exports resumed. But, apart from such exports, Russia's economic situation worsened. Its citizens and Eastern and Central European customers could not afford to pay world prices, or to pay in hard currency. So they were paying for oil by bartering goods, a procedure which, in turn, threw Russians out of work, too.

The result is that there is no money to replace equipment, repair it, or redeploy rigs that are consequently abandoned. Along the route to Gulf's oil-field operations, dozens of rigs have been left to rust for years because there's no budget for exploration. There is also no money to capture and pipeline the natural gas that is produced here. So flames as tall as two-storey houses burn off trillions of cubic feet of natural gas because there's no money to build a gas pipeline.

In North America, gas is recaptured and used to power the rigs. Here, rigs were run electrically, and power lines were strung hundreds of kilometres, even for a handful of preliminary wells. The region was fuelled totally by power from a nearby nuclear reactor, not by the plentiful natural gas that was obtainable a few kilometres away.

"Under their system they would tell the bureaucracy how many wells they were going to drill in the next two years and order whatever they needed from rigs to power lines," explained Guthrie. "But even if they found nothing after their first few wells, they would continue to drill the rest because that was the plan and they had to stick to it. In Canada, two dry holes and you move."

THE FUTURE

At a fruit market in Kiev, Ukraine, I asked my translator to negotiate the purchase of lemons, out of courtesy so that my photographer-companion, Norm Betts, could take a photograph of the lemon vendor. She bargained with the man and said to me, "It's outrageous. He wants a dollar apiece."

I asked her what the lemons were worth, and she said a fraction of that amount. I then instructed her to give the man 25 cents. It was still excessive, but a small price to pay for the pose. Once the picture was taken, we turned our backs, but the translator remained with the vendor. I saw him hand her two more lemons, which she promptly put into her purse. When she noticed me staring at her, she blushed and apologized. I said to her, "Don't apologize. You just became a broker. Buyer and seller were happy and you deserved something extra for your efforts."

The anecdote illustrates how cunning — and capitalistic — Eastern Europeans already are. Their communist system strangled initiative and punished enterprise, but the people merely went underground or "worked on the left," as they described black-market activities. Everyone cheated, and most got away with it. Now the cheating is out in the open. But the people resent this in a way because their cradle-to-grave security has disappeared with the hyperinflation of the ruble. They would have preferred to keep getting their state paycheques and moonlight to supplement them.

When trying to speculate as to what will happen in the former Soviet Union, one must concede the fact that the communists did some things better than many capitalist societies have done: they eradicated illiteracy and created one of the world's most educated workforces. Half of the world's engineers and one-third of its doctorates live in the former Soviet Union. And the future is bright indeed if their brain-power, freed from the need to devise weapons of destruction or defence, can be devoted to money-making pursuits such as the development of pharmaceuticals, industrial chemicals, new or better energy sources, and electronics. This won't happen overnight for the Soviets, but the value of human capital — along with mineral wealth — cannot be overestimated.

But, as usual, the impediment is politics. Russia or the other republics could be taken over by nationalists or military leaders — but that's doubtful. One aborted coup attempt in 1992 later, the Soviets are simply doing what they have always done. Ignoring their government, taking their pathetic paycheques for doing very little at work, and moonlighting. Whether factory labourers, KGB operatives, or army infantry, the Soviets are still a nation of sneaky, and sheep-like, people. For decades, they put up with, without mutiny, horrendous regimes that jailed them, murdered them, and lied to them. There's little or no evidence that they will lift a finger to move along changes, much less to stop those break-away provinces and cities who, I believe, will simply drift into uncontested new nationhood.

The spring 1993 referendum that kept Boris Yeltsin in power was a case in point. The majority said they trusted Yeltsin, who's been at loggerheads with the unelected congress of deputies for more than one year. But then the majority also voted against holding snap elections of the congress, which was, frankly, the only way to get them off Yeltsin's back and get on with the business of rapid reforms. The contradictory decisions, in essence, meant Russians did not want changes, even if the *status quo* meant a continuing deadlock in Moscow.

In keeping with the Russian adage "the government pretends to pay us and we pretend to work," the people are satisfied with life as usual without the police state. Eventually, they will create a form of market economy, but it will take years. In the meantime, Western Europeans will lend them money, amid fears of collapse and mass migration, but will stop short of a financing a Marshall Plan. The Americans, once the missiles and nuclear armaments are completely destroyed, will leave matters up to the Europeans. In the meantime, or until rules change to encourage enterprise, the Russians, Ukrainians, and others will simply get on with the business of getting by. One day, perhaps, they may also get ahead.

THE MIDDLE
EAST AND
AFRICA

HE COLLAPSE OF THE RUSSIAN EMPIRE CREATED MANY
casualties beyond its borders, notably in those vas-
sal countries dependent upon Soviet largesse during
the Cold War. Marxist regimes in Angola,
Zimbabwe, Zambia and elsewhere have abandoned
the communist cause in the absence of continuing
financial support from Moscow. Cuba struggles. Now they
must seek help from others or the United Nations or, as is
mostly the case, do without much aid at all. Finding bene-
factors is made more difficult as aid is being used more and
more to facilitate trade. Some European countries have begun
to count as "foreign aid" loans extended by their export-
import banks to countries for the purpose of buying

European products and services. Even Canada has begun to divert aid from African countries (which used to receive nearly half of all foreign aid granted by Canada) to areas where Canada's strategic trade interests lie — Eastern Europe, Latin America, and China. As industrialized countries suffer from slow growth themselves, many feel they must dole out aid where it will most likely yield trade opportunities.

While Russia's problems are indeed daunting, other outcasts — Africa and the Middle East — have even less hope for prosperity in the medium or long run unless they form their own regional trading blocs. There are several natural ones already being discussed, but these arrangements are in their infancy, and much depends on external and internal problems being sorted out first. And problems are daunting. Most African and Middle East countries suffer from a deadly combination of tyranny, overpopulation, and ignorance. Their leaders currently spend too much money on themselves and on arms, and spend too little on education and enterprise.

However misguided they are, their needs cannot be ignored by the world. The more outcast nations are isolated, economically speaking, the worse off we will all be: like bad neighbourhoods in a city, these countries are breeding-grounds for poverty, pollution, and crimes of an international magnitude. The worst example thus far was Saddam Hussein's attempted theft of an entire country, Kuwait. This attempted "hold-up" sparked a United Nations police action, called the Gulf War, which cost the rest of the world $73.2 billion in 1991, and billions more since because Hussein was neither captured nor removed. Then, in 1992, Somalia erupted, and U.S. troops, then U.N. troops, were sent at great expense to control local warlords who were intercepting food aid intended for the people. Months and billions of dollars later, the soldiers were still there. And there will be more Husseins and more Somalias in the future. These countries are the world's mean streets — dangerous for anyone to visit and quite capable of exporting violence beyond their borders. These countries are also frightening. Many have nuclear weapons — for example, North Korea or Pakistan — and may not hesitate to use them. Worse than being shut out of the Triad, many countries (mostly in Africa) appear to be incapable of helping themselves get ahead.

The Middle East tinderbox — once a tug-of-war between superpowers during the Cold War — is still volatile because talks between Israel and its Moslem enemies have yielded very little in the way of results after many months. Israel, frightened of rejection by its U.S. ally, asked in 1993 to be part of the North American Free Trade Agreement. "A bilateral agreement between us already exists, but we want to be a full-fledged member along with Canada and Mexico in the expanded version of the agreement," said Israeli foreign minister Shimon Peres in an interview in spring 1993.

Israel and others continue to be terrorist targets in the absence of any resolution of the Palestinian question. Attacks against tourists in Egypt were stepped up, beginning in 1992, to punish it for its continued recognition of Israel, with the result that the country has been deprived of needed revenue. New York's World Trade Center was severely damaged by a terrorist bomb in 1993, set by Islamic fanatics. And Iranian fundamentalists have been opening mosques in former Soviet republics populated by Moslems. To gain converts, their leaders have been preaching outright hatred and inciting a call to arms against the Russians and others. Meanwhile,

Africa remained in a sorry state, with the awful distinction that it was the only region in the world where incomes at the end of the 1980s were lower than at the decade's beginning.

THE NASTY NUCLEAR CLUB

South Africa's white regime shocked the world in 1993 by admitting, after years of denial, that it had developed eight nuclear devices. But, the announcement added, these weapons had been destroyed. The reason was obvious. As whites braced themselves for the inevitability of black majority rule, they were distinctly unwilling to hand over nuclear weapons to the black majority.

South Africa is now accepted, but the world may grow more dangerous as a result of the demise of the Cold War unless nuclear arms are carefully guarded. If not, terrorism will become potentially more lethal. Psychotic leaders with nuclear warheads may be able to extort or hold up entire nations. Terrorist acts around the world continue, perpetuated by poor, landless people or those with unrequited land claims, such as the PLO, IRA, and certain Islamic fundamentalist groups. Just as exports are freer in the global economy, so is the export of violence and terrorism as the movement of people and goods flow readily in an increasingly borderless world.

Besides the new world disorder has forced millions to look for another line of work. That is why it was a worrying sight to land in Kiev, Ukraine, in February 1992 and see planes on the tarmac mostly from Moslem nations such as Iraq, Iran, Kuwait, Libya, and Algeria. Entry to the sixth floor of my hotel was restricted because the Iranian government had leased the premises for at least one year. A Ukrainian cabinet minister said in an interview that his government had signed an oil-pipeline deal with Iran for strategic reasons. The strategy was to make Ukraine less dependent upon Russia, which supplied all of Ukraine's oil and natural gas. But such cosiness between a nuclear powerhouse like Ukraine and troublesome nations like Iran or Iraq and the others was worrisome.

By 1993, Ukraine felt like an outcast twice over. It shunned its former Soviet partners and was shunned by the West too. So a controversy in 1993 over the dismantling of its weapons — despite its self-professed goal of total nuclear disarmament — underscored how the world's neediest orphans can create problems for everyone unless they are helped. Desperate nations, like desperate people, are extremely dangerous.

In early 1993, Russia and the United States ballyhooed the signing of a sweeping disarmament treaty dubbed START-2. Months later, my Ukrainian contacts informed me that the Ukrainian parliament had still refused to ratify the arms-cutting treaty's forerunner, START-1. START-2 was conditional upon START-1's execution.

What concerned me most was that Ukraine's stubbornness delayed START-2, which aimed to destroy two-thirds of all missiles in the United States and the former Soviet Union. It concerned the Americans too. Months after the ballyhooing, neither treaty was worth the paper it was written on.

START-2 was signed with indecent haste by outgoing president George Bush and an equally desperate Russian president Boris Yeltsin for political reasons. The treaty was not ratified, however, by the other three members of the former Soviet nuclear club — Ukraine, Byelorussia, and Kazakhstan, each of which has dozens of deadly long-range missiles in silos. Ukraine politicians were balking at ratification in part because of the huge expense involved, as well as for security reasons. Both concerns were valid, but the United States refused to address them.

Ukraine was worried about Russia and had sound historical reasons to be. The last thing that allies should have wanted was for Russia to have the upper hand once again over a defanged Ukraine, Byelorussia, and Kazakhstan because that would make possible the re-establishment of the old Russian Empire, or the Soviet Union. Ukraine and the others were holding out for non-aggression guarantees from their old oppressor, Russia, as well as for firm promises that they would come under NATO's military protection, like Poland and other Eastern-bloc nations.

Dismantling the huge intercontinental ballistic missiles will cost billions. The treaties with the United States promise U.S. aid to help defray the costs, but revenue-sharing arrangements between Moscow and Ukraine, Byelorussia, and Kazakhstan have not been discussed. This is critical to Ukraine because, for instance, in 1992 Russia collected Ukraine's tactical nuclear weapons (movable battlefield weapons), then turned around and sold to the United States fissionable nuclear material from these weapons without sharing the proceeds. Some Ukrainians then argued that their weapons should be swapped only in return for a pledge of protection from Russia and US$1.5 billion in direct compensation. Dismantling estimates are high because of the delicate and difficult nature of the operation and incumbent restoration expenses accruing from the environmental damage around the silos.

Ukraine's stubbornness was also understandable in light of the fact that the United States had not recognized Ukraine and the others as fully independent, free-standing Eastern European democracies that just happened to border Russia. The so-called Confederation of Independent States is toothless. It amounts essentially to wishful thinking on the part of the Russians.

The most annoying aspect of Washington's persistence in signing disarmament, debt, and aid deals with Moscow alone was that it also overlooked the significance of Ukraine's unilateral declaration of independence in August 1991 in unravelling the fearsome Soviet Union. Ukraine's departure was, by many accounts, the nail in the Soviet Union's coffin, and yet Ukraine has been insensitively, if not cavalierly, dealt with by both superpowers. Still annoying to Ukrainians was President Bush's notorious "Chicken Kiev" speech in Ukraine's parliament in August 1991, right after its declaration of independence, in which Bush urged the country to reconsider its decision to leave the Soviet fold. Imagine a U.S. president actually wanting to prop up the former Soviet Union!

Fortunately, Canada (with one million Ukrainian Canadians) is Ukraine's natural ally and went to bat for it during closed-door debt discussions within the G-7. Germany, owed the lion's share of the former Soviet debt of some US$62 billion, insisted that no fresh loans be advanced until Ukraine signed loan agreements that would force it to be on the hook for any outstanding loans if Russia and others were unable to pay them. Eventually a new, fairer debt-repayment agreement was negotiated, but fell apart in December 1992, because Russia would not also disclose or deal with the division of assets, such as foreign reserves, real estate, and other valuables. A tentative deal dividing debts and assets was announced in early 1993, but cynics suspect it may fall apart too.

The world must worry that Ukraine or some of its citizens may flee into the arms of questionable parties like Iran. Fortunately, measures have been taken to employ some of Ukraine's nuclear scientists, many of whom now work for a U.S.–funded institute in Kiev dedicated to helping clean up the nuclear-reactor mess in that country. Clearly, the institute is designed to keep tabs on scientists and to keep them off the payroll of unfriendly nations such as Iran or Libya. But there's little that can stop someone from being enticed away by some despot who wants his own nuclear bombs.

Fortunately, this controversy over the START treaty controversy has focused more attention on the fact that Ukraine and the others are still locked in a potentially dangerous Russian vice. Unable to negotiate direct compensation for disarmament, Ukraine and the others must rely on the largesse of their former enemy, which has been less than generous thus far. Unable to meet its own energy needs, Ukraine's attempts to build a pipeline from the Middle East have been frustrated as Russia refuses to grant an easement for the line through a portion of its territory. Ukraine and the others must be truly independent if peace is to last in that region. Put another way, if their current predicament isn't overcome, their problems may end up becoming a bigger worry for us all.

That controversy aside, there are still many indications that armaments, and even nuclear materials, are being bought and sold surreptitiously by unemployed military men or government officials. Indications are that the Croats and

Serbs have obtained their weapons from the Russian military, either legally or secretly. Frightening to me was a first-hand account of a smuggling attempt. "I was called up the other day," Canadian businessman Geoffrey Carr-Harris said in an interview, "and offered a vial of red mercury for US$5 million."

Red mercury is an essential ingredient in making an atom bomb, and its possession is highly regulated, except in the former Soviet Union. It must be remembered that, while the Soviets lived in third-world conditions, their education was first rate. Ukraine, only 15 per cent of the empire, had an aerospace program the size of France's. In fact, it could be larger, but no one knows for sure. Entire cities were off limits to Russians or others, walled to keep people within, because industries were conducting top-secret research or manufacture of items for military use. While some Soviet technology was backward, much was not. After the empire collapsed, it appeared that everything was for sale to the highest bidder, no matter what the buyer's motive or what passport he carried. The outcasts are a nuclear-size worry to the rest of the world.

THE MOSLEM OUTCASTS

One of the most interesting possibilities as the new world evolves is the emergence of a new super-region made up of 10 bordering Moslem nations. Now adrift, they are attempting to form another important trading bloc in competition with the Triad. Members of this Islamic bloc include the six former Soviet republics of Central Asia — Uzbekistan, Tajikistan, Azerbaijan, Kyrghyzstan, Turkmenistan, and

Kazakhstan. Each is an independent country, and all six undoubtedly hope to wean themselves from any dependence upon their former master and oppressor, Russia. That was, in part, why they joined forces, in a preliminary way, with their Moslem brethren in Turkey, Iran, Pakistan, and Afghanistan. In November 1992, these 10 nations formed the Economic Cooperation Organization (ECO) and, perhaps symbolically, straddle the Silk Road that linked Asia and Europe in ancient times.

These nations have much in common. Their people are of Moslem background and their native tongues are comprehensible to one another because each is a derivation of Turkish. The Silk Road and its wealth attracted acquisitors such as Ghenghis Khan, Great Britain, and finally Russia.

Even today, the 10 collectively have much going for them. The six ex-Soviet Central Asian nations have oil, gold, mineral wealth, forests, and agriculture. They also have a well-educated workforce, unlike the four non-Soviet members of the new organization. Iran has enormous oil wealth and, like the four non-Soviet nations, a young, low-cost labour force. The six former Soviet republics have 50 million people, including 10 million Russian ethnics. The other four have a combined population of 250 million. The bloc could be powerful and influential.

The ECO was born in Islamabad in 1992 out of the ashes of the Cold War. Pakistan, Iran, Turkey, and Afghanistan each feared the Soviets, and that common fear led them to form various alliances. In forming the ECO, they simply merged the various pacts and extended them to include the other members. The Turks, the capitalist leaders of the group, were interested in such a bloc because they had been continuously rejected by the European Community. Many feel

Turkey, "the poor man of Europe," has been denied entry because it is not a Christian nation. Attacks against Turkish workers in Germany and Arabs in France, and Europe's unwillingness to save Bosnia and its Moslems from an illegal invasion by Serbs and Croats, underscored to many what appears to be Europe's racism.

The benefits of the ECO notwithstanding, there are problems to overcome. Iran has been exporting extremists to set up radical mosques that rail against the Russians and Christians. At the November 1992 meeting to set up the ECO, reports said that Iran argued for a purely Islamic bloc — a sort of bigoted trading bloc — as an alternative to the European community. But Turkey and Pakistan were cool to the notion, undoubtedly because Turkey enjoys a huge trade surplus with the European Community and, if forced to choose, would probably opt to join Europe. Interestingly, Russia announced in the spring of 1993 its hope to join the group. If allowed to join — and it may be partly a defensive manoeuvre to protect the 10 million Russians in the Central Asian republics — Russia will ensure that the trading bloc will not become an intolerant religious bloc.

A trade and development bank was established at the inaugural ECO meeting, and a schedule of quarterly conferences was set to iron out tariff breaks and technology transfers. While the ECO is a good idea, it has many problems. Most of the nations involved are poor and sell many of the same products. And the group's leader, Turkey, the only semi-industrialized country, is not exactly a powerhouse itself. There are also security worries about Iraq, a regressive Russia, and many land disputes with China. Much money must be spent to build infrastructure, and some members are so poor that payment for imports may be possible only through barter, a difficult and undesirable prospect.

The biggest impediment of all is the fact that Islamic fundamentalism precludes wealth creation in a capitalist sense. Lending and interest payments are considered immoral by fundamentalists, which, quite frankly, prevents the accumulation of capital necessary for economic growth. Women become second-class citizens, which cuts the workforce in half and usually results in overpopulation. For example, oil-rich Moslem states have mostly missed the opportunity to create industrial societies as a result of the ban on usury. Unable to collect interest within their countries, they invested outside them. Instead of creating enterprises at home, they used their oil wealth to buy luxury items, build fancy infrastructure, educate and house their people, and acquire arms.

But so-called secular Moslem countries like Malaysia and Indonesia are fast-growing and, along with Turkey, represent important role models for modern nations. Indications are that the six Central Asian states are irreligious, having let their religion die in the atheist Soviet Union. Besides, they are considerably more interested in market reforms and trade than in settling any old scores concerning the Palestinians, Israelis, and others in the Middle East. These festering, and unsolved, problems still preoccupy Iran and the Arab Moslem nations.

Those concerned about a Moslem monolith say signs point away from religious fanaticism. They point out that not one of the six new countries has chosen to switch to an Arabic alphabet from the Cyrillic alphabet of Russian. Most have abandoned Russian as an official language and opted for their Turkish dialects instead, adopting along with it the Roman alphabet used in Turkey. This would indicate that they want mostly to turn their orientation toward the west, not the east or the south.

THE MIDDLE EAST

The Middle East is no longer strategically important, now that the Cold War has ended, but it remains financially important because more than half of the world's cheap crude-oil reserves are there. That is why the Gulf War was fought in 1991: Saddam Hussein's invasion of Kuwait gave him leverage, and possibly a military advantage, over the entire Persian Gulf region. And, if any single individual controlled the region, he could control the world's economy, ratcheting inflation rates up and down merely by moving the price of exported crude oil. He would have become a one-man OPEC.

Hussein was humiliated in that war and driven back to Baghdad. The U.S. victory also won it an important seat at what's left of the OPEC oil cartel. The United States was built on cheap crude oil, but supplies are quickly running dry. During the 1980s, the United States went from importing less than it produced to importing more than it produced. The change has cost it billions of dollars annually. As the world's biggest oil-buyer, Washington simply could not let Hussein or anyone else dictate crude prices to the world. After the Gulf War, the Arab oil states owe the United States plenty. OPEC is defanged, perhaps forever. Some OPEC members, such as Ecuador and eventually Venezuela, are drifting away from the oil cartel to please the thirsty United States. Both those countries, are trying to curry Washington's favour to gain access to America's free-trade zone.

The Gulf War, while successful in pushing Hussein out of Kuwait, left many problems unresolved in the region. Israel is still enmeshed in talks with its hostile Arab neighbours over the possible creation of a homeland for the Palestinians. Violence continues around the world. Hussein is still alive and well, and stirring up trouble once in a while. Iran exports fundamentalist hatred.

The Palestinian problem nags as Israelis debate the issues involved, such as security and costs of handing over part of their country to create a Palestinian homeland. Both sides have legitimate claims. The creation of Israel in 1948 did not lead to an expulsion of Arabs, but certain elements made them feel unwelcome. And rather than create a country tolerant of all those residing there, Israelis adopted Jewish law and Hebrew as the only official language. The intolerance on the part of some Israelis fanned the flames of fundamentalists. So did Israel's enormous economic and military success. It stands alone in this dangerous region as a first world country with a mature democracy, educated populace, and modern industrialized economy. The real tragedy is Israel and its neighbours could form another powerful trading bloc, but they seem incapable of resolving their differences. Instead, Iran seeks alliances with other Moslem nations, and Israel seeks closer ties to North America or Europe.

Israel aside, the Middle East will remain volatile because 10 million Arabs have fabulous wealth and centuries' worth of crude oil left, while 300 million live in utter poverty nearby. They are running out of water and arable soil as the spreading desert claims both. The Arab nations plus Iran occupy 13 million square kilometres of the Earth's surface, and about 89 per cent of it is desert. "Of the [remaining] 11 per cent, they will lose one-quarter in the coming seven years to desert," said Israeli foreign minister Shimon Peres in an interview in early 1993. "It is tragic. This is an announcement about starvation. And we cannot take out the violence in this land unless we answer the call of the stomach."

If peace is ever achieved between Israel and its enemies, Israeli technology and brainpower could be harnessed to help convert desert back into arable lands. "We should organize a campaign against the desertification of the land. There is also the organization of available water. Waters are not disciplined by politics. They move in the belly of the land. Rains don't go through customs. We took a land that was a desert and use one-third as much water as others," said Peres.

Israel quietly lends such expertise to its only Middle East ally, Egypt, but keeps this close to its vest because of fears of reprisals. Already, Egypt and the United States have been the victims of stepped-up terrorism in 1993 as talks with Israel fell apart.

AFRICA

North Africa suffers from the grim effects of desertification and overpopulation. With the exception of relatively democratic Egypt, this region's people are controlled by tyrants or monarchs. Libya's Muammar Qaddafi has financed the terrorist adventures of the PLO and the IRA for decades, but failed to lift the educational or economic level of his people. Somalia, Ethiopia, and others have been preoccupied with feeding their populace. Countries ringing North Africa's desert fall prey to its spread. Every year, the Sahara Desert grows by up to 160 kilometres, swallowing up lands used for cattle grazing. As the desert impinges and winds make the dust airborne, the formation of clouds is impeded, thus spreading the desert farther faster. Desertification is a problem throughout the north and, increasingly, the centre of the continent.

Africa's principal problem, however, is that, decades after most of its nations have gained postwar independence, they have not replaced the entrepreneurs, such as East Indians or Europeans, that many African nations expelled. The exploitative colonial systems imposed by most European countries did not lift the locals into the twentieth century with the result that corruption, imperfect democracies, hobbled news-media, and tribal rivalries have afflicted the Dark Continent ever since.

As the problems of poverty and conflict proliferate, they also add to the woes of the only engine of economic growth that exists in sub-Sahara Africa — industrialized South Africa. Millions flood into its crowded townships, or squatters' camps, on the outskirts of its biggest cities — Johannesburg, Durban, and Cape Town. This deluge has been caused by the rescinding of the Pass Laws that restricted movements within the country by blacks, so many have gone to the cities to rejoin breadwinners or seek jobs. More recently, the collapse of Angola's Marxist regime and Mozambique's continuing civil war have led to mass migration of refugees out of those countries and into the teeming camps of South Africa.

This is of great concern to southern Africa in general. It must be remembered that, even during the despicable apartheid system, South Africa's black-ruled neighbours, such as Botswana, Mozambique, Zimbabwe, and Zambia, refused to join in any of the world's trade sanctions against the oppressive white regime and did business readily with the whites. Such tolerance was necessary because the region depends on South Africa's superb railway and port systems to get products in and out of the sub-Sahara. Besides, South Africa was the only African source for many consumer or industrial goods sought by Africans and their governments and enterprises.

Concern is that South Africa's whites may obstruct black majority rule, which would result in widespread bloodshed, or that the country may deteriorate into internecine conflict between black factions after the whites eventually hand over control. Southern Africa needs a strong, united South Africa if the continent is ever to have a trading bloc of any consequence.

SOUTH AFRICA

Apartheid truly ended as the Cold War wound down. In February 1989, South Africa's president Frederik de Klerk legitimized the African National Congress and released black leader Nelson Mandela, who had endured 27 years' imprisonment. Three years later, in March 1992, de Klerk sought a renewed mandate from white votes. They voted 68.7 per cent in favour of negotiating a new constitution that would give the vote to blacks for the first time in South Africa's history.

These about-faces occurred because South Africa's apartheid became another Cold War casualty. Sanctions over the years did not destroy its evil, racist system. The world boycotted South Africa way back in March 1960 after the bloody Sharpeville riots. But, it was decades later, after the disappearance of the Iron Curtain thousands of kilometres to its north, that whites in South Africa began to surrender their evil system.

Apartheid survived sanctions because for years the United States turned a blind eye on the injustice of the system. South African whites fought communist regimes in Angola and Mozambique. Tellingly, South Africa was supplied with arms and other materiel by Israel throughout the period of sanctions; probably, Israel acted as a proxy for Washington, offering an indirect way for the Pentagon to get around the sanctions. There were other telltale incidents, such as the mysterious leniency exhibited by U.S. Customs officials toward exports to South Africa by Canadian weapons expert the late Gerald Bull. The easy passage of those weapons was well-documented. So was the involvement of South Africans in Irangate — the U.S. guns-for-hostages fiasco.

But, after the collapse of the Iron Curtain, the United States no longer needed a fierce anti-communist ally. Angola, Zimbabwe, and Mozambique abandoned their Marxist ways, and, with the communist threat gone, white South Africans also began to grumble about military conscription and huge army expenditures.

Negotiations to work out a new sharing arrangement with the blacks began after the 1992 referendum, but stalled because of violence between black factions and white police brutality. The white government was also reluctant to turn everything over immediately to the black majority, amid fears that their leaders would wreck the country's industrial and resource base. Besides, by 1992, South Africa was spending US$1,520 a year on the education of white students, US$1,140 on Indian students, US$950 on coloured or mixed-race students, and only US$380 on black kids. Power-sharing meant an immediate and massive transfer of entitlements from the white minority to the black and coloured majority.

Around this time, political troubles and slumping gold and diamond prices began to put the country into decline. Ironically, the fate of other blacks in southern Africa hinged on the success of whites. South Africa was the only first-world economy on the Dark Continent, with a gross national product equivalent to that of all the sub-Sahara. It had become the engine driving much of Africa's economy. Botswana, for instance, derived 16 per cent of its gross national product from the wages sent home by Botswana breadwinners working in South Africa's mines.

Without mining and manufacturing, South Africa's newly freed blacks would inherit no spoils. Worse yet, crumbling economies in neighbouring countries had led to mass migration into South Africa's already crowded shantytowns. Durban, on the Indian Ocean, had become the world's fastest-growing city by 1992. The hillsides and outskirts of all South Africa's cities — from Johannesburg to scenic Cape Town — were littered with squatters' camps where families lived in tents or shacks roofed with plastic held down by bricks and boards. Crime was rampant, and so was violence in the cities.

As Marxist regimes brought economic collapse in Zimbabwe, Angola, and Zambia, people streamed south, then turned to market reforms too late, after the Soviet Union had disappeared. Anarchy and civil war in Mozambique and elsewhere resulted in a flood of uninvited refugees into South Africa's economy, as happened in Germany and Europe. This deluge surpassed the flood to the cities after the hated Pass Laws were abolished in 1986.

The result was that, by 1992, South Africa had become the world's most genteel armed camp. Whites continued to enjoy an exceptionally privileged existence. A drug-store owner could afford two servants, a fancy house, clubs, safaris, and a life of leisure because he paid starvation wages to the help. Black servants made $75 a month plus room and board, or roughly the cost of three rounds of golf at a Johannesburg country club. But whites were armed to the teeth. Joggers carried pistols. Downtown shopping malls were armed fortresses. Razor wire surrounded homes, schools, and factories. Purses were routinely searched at entrances to hotels and offices. Roads were clogged with taxi-vans so commuters could avoid trains, where machete-wielding terrorists had slaughtered hundreds.

Whites still enjoyed reasonable lifestyles, but martial law was imposed in black shantytowns like Soweto (the acronym for Southwest Township). The squalor was a ticking time bomb. Officially, Soweto's population was 1.5 million, but unofficially some guessed it to be 5 million or more. At dusk, when the wind picked up smoke from millions of coal stoves in Soweto and the squatters' camps beyond, motorists for several kilometres along the bordering highways were blinded and choked.

As the country marched toward true democracy, there were notable holdouts. In a dusty town two hours outside Johannesburg squatted the headquarters of neo-Nazi Eugene Terre-Blanche, whose Huguenot name means "white land." Terre-Blanche's office is decorated with near-swastikas, and men in brown shirts looking distinctly like Hitlerian henchmen mill around the place. The reality of Africa is now what it was in ancient times: eat or be eaten. It's the law of the jungle, and one still subscribed to by Africans, both black and white. When it comes to gluttony and ferocity, no tribe on the Dark Continent has outperformed the white Africans of this wealthy land. "We paid for this country in blood and tears," Terre-Blanche said in an interview in June 1992. "Black and white cannot govern together, so we are preparing for the coming revolution by training our people."

He claimed to have 15,000 uniformed men prepared to do what the Rhodesians did in 1965 when whites refused to accede to the black majority, opted out of the British empire, and waged civil war for 15 years against black liberation parties. Outnumbered 25 to 1, they held out against world opinion, international sanctions, and black guerrillas before handing over the country to socialists who called the country Zimbabwe. After the civil war, 200,000 of Rhodesia's 300,000 whites left. Whites in South Africa are outnumbered 6 to 1, but haven't anywhere else to go.

Even if South Africa avoids a white–black conflict, the country may deteriorate into a civil war of black against black, as happened in Zimbabwe after the whites surrendered control. It all depends on whether or not two princes representing two distinct tribes in South Africa can make peace.

Nelson Mandela, a Xhosa (KoSa) prince, and Zulu prince Mangosuthu Buthelezi are fierce enemies. Mandela, a martyr because of his 27 years in prison, is destined to become the country's first black president, even though Buthelezi represents the largest black tribe, the Zulus.

Mandela's biggest task may be how he deals with the Zulus, not the whites. His own party, the ANC, is littered with thugs and communists. Some Zulus are no better. In the summer of 1992, terrible massacres by both factions received world headlines and brought negotiations for a new constitution to a halt for many months.

Unlike Mandela and his ANC, Buthelezi bills himself as a

moderate Christian free-enterpriser. But he has been snubbed in constitutional talks, and the ANC maintains he's not the Martin Luther King Jr. of South Africa but a modern version of Shaka, the legendary, ruthless Zulu chief. Cunning and crazy, Shaka sacrificed 7,000 Zulus in his grief after his mother died. Buthelezi has also been tainted because he accepted funding for his independent homeland from the hated white regime. Unfortunately, he represents 8 million Zulus, and unless they are given a place in the new black majority government, there will be more trouble even when the blacks get what they have long deserved.

CONCLUSION

The outcasts of the world must form alliances that will help them economically if they are unable to become members of the Triad. But, joining the rich countries' clubs is not easy, as Mexico discovered in its protracted talks with the United States over free trade. Global restructuring has rocked the economies of wealthy countries, causing many of them to become protectionist and preoccupied with their own problems. At the same time, a handful of worrisome tyrants has emerged — some with nuclear weapons and some without — who may decide that their situations are so hopeless that the only way they can advance their countries' ambitions is by conquest or terrorism.

Fortunately, the majority of countries simply want to make ends meet, and have no ambitions beyond their own borders. Just as black African nations held their noses and traded with South Africa's hated apartheid regime, orphan countries are searching for new trading partners wherever they can. But the best hope of all rests in further liberalization of all world trade for the benefit of all nations through revisions to GATT. Trade, and aid, are mankind's best hope, and represent the only fair and meaningful social safety net in a world that may otherwise become very, very dangerous.

CANADA IN THE
TWENTY-FIRST
CENTURY

ANADA MUST REINVENT ITSELF IN ORDER TO MAINTAIN
its living standards in the twenty-first century. That
does not mean that Canada must become a sweatshop or scrap its health system. However, Canadians
must dismantle, restructure, and reduce the size of
their public sector to cut deficits and taxes. While
such an undertaking is difficult, Canada is luckier than most
countries who must perform major surgery on their society
and economy. After all, unlike the United States, Canadian
streets are safe. Unlike vast portions of the world, we are
not plagued with ethnic or religious clashes. Canadians are
well fed, well housed, and relatively well educated; our free-
enterprise system is first class; our infrastructure is in place

and well maintained; our principal trade access is guaranteed under the Free Trade Agreement; and our legal system fair and honest.

Unfortunately, Canada cannot pass the baton of high living standards to future generations in the next century without making drastic reforms.

AVERTING CANADA'S DEBT CRISIS

One dark day in 1982, the Mexican middle class was wiped out financially. The banks closed and, when they reopened, the peso had been calamitously devalued, brought down by excessive government debts. Every depositor had his or her savings reduced overnight to a fraction of their original value. To boot, the government nationalized the entire banking system that day in order to stop a disastrous run by depositors, which would have brought down the country's domestic financial system. Mexico took this drastic action because its politicians had overspent, counting on ever-increasing oil prices, and borrowed too much from foreign lenders to do so. The country's debts were equivalent to more than twice its GDP or total economic size — a threshold of no return, by the way, that Canada will reach in the 1990s at the current rate of deficit spending.

Canada's collective government debt was $630 billion by March 1993. At an average rate of 7 per cent interest the debt will double by 2003, to $1.26 trillion, even if budgets were balanced. By contrast, the Canadian GDP of $700 billion in 1993 — growing at 2 per cent average per year compounded — will not double until 2029. Worse yet, if interest rates increase or deficits continue (they will be an estimated

$55 billion in the fiscal year 1993–94), the doubling takes place sooner. Even if interest rates stay level and budgets are balanced, the $1.26-trillion debt will double again, to $2.52 trillion, or nearly four times the economy's size, by 2013. Obviously, massive inflation will occur, then currency devaluation. This is the Mexican meltdown scenario.

Of course, Mexico never went bust. Countries don't actually go out of business. But the pain was enormous. Individuals and corporations went bust. Many others fled before disaster struck. And the damage — even after debts are restructured and partially paid off or forgiven — lingers. Some 11 years after Mexico's crisis in 1982, that country's middle class was still playing catch-up to the 1970s, in terms of peso buying power. Its underclass suffered even more, as its economy shrank and failed to create jobs for the unskilled or new entrants into its workforce. Illegal migration to the United States reached unprecedented levels, estimated to be 1.5 million per year. A brain drain, and an estimated $38 billion, left Mexico.

Mexico spent nearly four years negotiating with 500 lenders from around the world, eventually signing a massive package in 1988 to stretch out loan payments and swap loans for long-term Mexican government bonds. Then began a rigorous process of fiscal restraint and revolutionary policy changes. Mexico was forced to abandon its isolationist past and join GATT. With his country open for business, newly elected president Carlos Salinas de Gortari toured the capitals, looking for opportunities and alliances. He was given the cold shoulder. The joke, often repeated in Mexico, was that "Salinas got breakfast in Washington, lunch in Tokyo, tea in Germany, but absolutely no interest in trade." That's when he requested membership to the handiest Triad member — the United States and Canada. Salinas realized he had to get inside one of the world's protective trade tents or end up one of the world's economic outcasts.

Mexico also had to get its macroeconomic house in order to strengthen the value of the peso. Currency stability was essential in order to attract the foreign investors or lenders who were needed to rebuild the country's third-world infrastructure and industries. Mexico also paid off foreign debts by undertaking one of the world's most ambitious, privatization programs.

Canada's crisis — when it comes — won't last as long as Mexico's has for two reasons. Canada is considerably richer than Mexico, with incredible underlying value in terms of its resources, land mass, and world-class infrastructure. These can be sold to pay down debts. Also, the United States would never allow Canada to decline: Americans have more money invested in Canada than in any other country in the world; Canada is the biggest single customer for U.S. goods and services in the world; and Wall Street holds more than half of Canada's foreign debt. An impaired or nearly bankrupt Canada would severely hurt the U.S. economy, and the U.S. Treasury would bail out Ottawa as it eventually did Mexico. Since Washington, in effect, backed Mexico's loan-swap arrangement because of concern about destabilization along its border, it would move immediately to shore up Canada if that was required.

Despite such backstopping, Canadians and their enterprises are already being eaten alive by compound interest. Brian Mulroney's government fortunately held the deficit for nine years to less than the rate of economic growth. But the federal portion still doubled as the provinces ran huge deficits. Roughly $1 out of every $3 collected in taxes of all kinds in Canada goes toward interest payments on government debts.

Canadians must get out from under this burden before a crisis occurs. In fact, Canada's governments should examine Mexico's recent actions after its debt problem and implement its policies before the crisis.

Canada should become one of the world's tax havens - a goal which, if achieved, would encourage U.S. plants to move northward for the first time in history. This is not pie in the sky. Governments in Canada own many valuable assets that can be sold to pay off debts. For instance, Ontario and Quebec Hydro — the two largest enterprises in the country — should be sold, and would probably fetch $13 billion apiece by some guesstimates. More creative privatizations should be undertaken, such as the sale of the mint, museums, public buildings, Canadian National Railways, and Canada Post. Governments also own massive tracts of real estate that should be sold to pay off debts.

The Mexicans, Czechs, Poles, and Chinese have devised some creative methods to transform their socialized economies and thus permanently reduce government deficits. For instance, they have been auctioning off leases to operate everything from water-treatment plants to highways, bridges, ports, airports, prisons, police forces, ferries, and canals. Bidders can lease — not own outright — existing facilities, and can also tender to build new facilities. In Mexico, for instance, tenders to build highways or bridges are awarded on the basis of price paid as well as how quickly the asset will revert to government ownership. The higher the price paid and more rapid its return to the government, the better. This means bidders must calculate what levies or tolls they will charge the public for the use of the highway or bridge to determine how quickly they can recoup their capital plus a profit before turning the asset over to the government. At the same time, Mexico makes sure that the tolls are not exorbitant.

Most important, Canada should streamline itself. Like a flabby corporation in a competitive climate, this country has become inefficient and encumbered by unneeded bureaucracies, too many governments, and too many politicians. Ideally, the entire provincial-governmental layer should be eliminated, and the federal or local governments take up the slack. Britain and Italy, with considerably larger populations, govern with only two levels — federal and municipal. So does Taiwan, with 20 million people. At the very least, the four Atlantic provinces should become one province, and Manitoba, Saskatchewan, Alberta, the Northwest Territories, and Yukon should merge too. Besides excessive numbers of governments, there is far too much duplication. Some regions have, for instance, four layers of environmental regulation. The Senate should be scrapped. But Canadians must also scrap certain attitudes they cling to regarding the role of government in our lives and economy.

TOSSING OUT THE BOGEYMEN

Canadian politicians have succumbed in the past to special-interest lobbies or misguided parties that have promoted a number of bogus notions and models for development. One of the most damaging, and expensive, has been belief in an "industrial strategy." A clone of communist central planning, this philosophy maintains that by throwing enough money at a hinterland it will become a heartland or that by throwing enough money at a venture it will become successful. This same flawed logic afflicts the World Bank and the IMF, as well as regional-development initiatives in Canada. Attempts to artificially inseminate Canada's, or the world's, backward portions rarely work and have added tens of billions of dollars to the nation's debts.

Another damaging belief has been that foreign ownership is somehow insidious and a threat to sovereignty. This may be true for countries dominated by one or two transnationals, families, or princes. But Canada's foreign-ownership situation was never a threat. In fact, it was a blessing. And the failure to recognize that has damaged Canada's economy. But the economic nationalists made hay by bashing foreign investment and then by embarking on excessive, misguided public-enterprise schemes for political ends.

The results have been depressing, and we're all still paying for it. For example, by June 1993, Calgary oil producer Renaissance Energy Ltd. was worth virtually as much on the stock market as was gigantic Petro-Canada. Few people have ever heard of Renaissance, which started off in 1982 as a numbered company owned by two publicity-shy, talented Calgarians. Petro-Canada, on the other hand, is a household name: it was launched with great political fanfare in 1975 by the Liberals to become Canada's oil flagship. But the comparison of these two enterprises provides the most stunning example of the failure and waste that have accompanied most public enterprises in this country. It's a disgrace that Petro-Canada, for all its billions of dollars in taxpayer subsidies, is only slightly bigger than Renaissance, which has never received a single cent of taxpayers' money.

Of course, Canada's not the only country that has blown its brains out giving money to civil servants who don't understand the marketplace. And Petro-Canada is not the only misadventure. Most of Canada's public enterprises — from airlines to hydro utilities — have racked up billions of dollars in debts for us to pay for generations ahead. The same misadventures occurred in Mexico, France, and Britain. An estimated $800-billion worth of government enterprises around the world are on the block. That does not include the entire communist world whose incompetent public enterprises are slowly being sold to private interests.

Petro-Canada fans will argue that it and Canada's other public corporations cannot be judged by financial criteria because they serve public-policy purposes too. But it is precisely that excuse which highlights why it is doubly instructive to examine just how unnecessary Petro-Canada has been from any policy viewpoint. Renaissance, without any taxpayer subsidies, has achieved the goals that the Liberals claimed they wanted to achieve, such as securing Canada's oil supply, increasing Canadian ownership, and creating jobs and economic activity. By June 1993, Renaissance's shares had a market value of around $2.2 billion, while Petro-Canada's were worth $2.4 billion. While PetroCan is still bigger, Renaissance is remarkable.

Calgary oil men have hated Petro-Canada from the start, partly for partisan reasons — Tory versus Liberal or socialist. But the national oil company, armed with policy objectives others were meeting and Ottawa's purse, went on a spree needlessly. For reasons unique to Canada, there was absolutely never any need to worry about foreign ownership of any resources, much less a need to create a national oil company. In essence, Petro-Canada was a colossal waste of taxpayers' money; too much was spent to buy resources already owned by Canadians.

Unlike the situation in the United States, in Canada most resources are retained by the "crown," or in other words are publicly owned. For instance, the lion's share of Canadian oil and natural-gas deposits are in Alberta, and the subsurface mineral rights — or actual resource ownership — on 80 per cent of the province's land mass belongs to the crown. The province leases these rights when they come up for renewal. Oil companies bid for them at regular auctions, and strings are attached. Big foreign companies cannot snap up all the leases and simply sit on the lands. Leases contain drilling rules and depth specifications, and always revert back to the crown after a period of time or if certain requirements have not been met.

Once oil or gas is discovered, the governments collect big royalties, even on so-called freehold lands where the subsurface mineral rights are owned by an individual farmer or landholder. About 20 per cent of Alberta is freehold; these lands were acquired by homesteaders before the territory joined confederation. But they pay a hefty extraction tax, too, on production. Lands sold after Alberta became a province include subsurface mineral rights. The same restriction is observed in the other western provinces.

Even so, on July 30, 1975, by act of Parliament, Petro-Canada was created by Ottawa to increase Canadian "ownership" in our oil industry; it then went on a buying spree with our money. In 1976, Atlantic Richfield Canada Ltd. was bought for $342 million; in 1978, Pacific Petroleums Ltd. for $1.496 billion; in 1981, Petrofina Canada Inc. for $1.46 billion; in 1983, BP Refinery and Marketing Canada Ltd. for $121.586 million; in 1985, Gulf Canada Ltd.'s gasoline stations for $611 million, and Norcen Energy Resources Ltd.'s Edmonton refinery for $301 million; and, in 1991,

Inter-City Gas Corporation's retail propane business for $235 million.

Those questionable acquisitions add up to more than $4.5 billion which, in 1990s dollars, would be more than double. Add to that, the constant losses over the years that Petro-Canada cost taxpayers and you have a king-sized billion-dollar boondoggle, on which taxpayers are still making interest payments.

Petro-Canada now is worth only slightly more than Renaissance, which began life in 1982 with a partnership between two Alberta farmboys, Ron Greene and Clayton Woitas. Greene came up through the business as a landman (he bids for leases and acquires freehold lands for drilling) and Woitas is a petroleum engineer. They put together a talented team which, through exploration, and not debt-financed buy-outs paid for by taxpayers, has found more oil and done more exploration than have giants like Petro-Canada. And these two Alberta farmboys have made their shareholders, government, employees, and suppliers rich doing so. Without costing any of us a dime, they have achieved the goals that Petro-Canada failed to achieve. Clearly, politicians and civil servants have absolutely no business in the world of business — not then, not now, and not ever.

In the 1990s, such nationalistic machismo is totally inappropriate. The mutual dependencies that arise out of the global economy, along with hundreds of other Petro-Canada scale–boondoggles, have contributed to one of the greatest attitudinal turn-arounds this century: by the 1980s, the foreign-owned transnational was being courted by every country, not reviled. Countries like India and Mexico opened wide their markets and joined the global economy. They dropped foreign-ownership restrictions and shamelessly courted investors. In a global economy, sovereignty was greatly eroded already anyway. National governments were becoming obsolete.

By 1990, there were 35,000 transnationals with 170,000 subsidiaries worldwide whose international savvy helped them to grow. Their success lies in adapting their goods and services to local needs while organizing their affairs to maximize use of global opportunities. The result is that about one-third of what the world called trade in 1990 was actually intercorporate transfers between these transnational subsidiaries operating in different countries. And the United Nation's figures showed that, in 1990, their combined sales, domestic and for export, were roughly twice the world's trade of US$2.2 trillion.

Transnationals make internal decisions that affect trade figures, currencies, and interest rates in the smaller or undeveloped countries in which they operate. This led many to fear them, amid speculation that transnationals could one day replace governments. Back in the 1970s, Wharton School of Business professor Howard Perlmutter made dire predictions that an oligopoly of 300 transnationals would control 80 per cent of the world's capital. By 1992, the top 100 corporations had acquired only 16 per cent of the world's total non-residential capital of US$20 trillion. The top 300 represented 24 per cent, according to *The Economist*.

But transnational power was overstated. Besides, transnationals are no longer the economic extensions of great military powers. In the past, Britain, the United States, France, and the others used gunboat diplomacy and armed force to protect corporate assets or business interests. Unspeakable regimes were propped up by national bullies to protect everything from Britain's opium trade in China to the CIA overthrow, after the Second World War, of Guatemala on behalf of U.S. interest in The United Fruit Company.

Those fears led some, like Mexico, to remain outside the global economy and not join the GATT process. It led many countries, including Canada, to adopt foreign-investment restrictions and to create large state enterprises to compete with the big European and U.S. transnationals. Canada, Mexico, Brazil, Angola, and dozens of others ended up wasting billions of tax dollars subsidizing crown corporations and state enterprises, amid concern that letting transnationals romp around freely in their economies would somehow result in a loss of sovereignty.

The reality was that sovereignty was slipping anyway for all countries as the world grew more interdependent. By the 1980s, government enterprises were being privatized by the hundreds, sold mostly to transnational subsidiaries, because they were inefficient and unable to survive against foreign competition. And as tariff barriers relentlessly came down postwar through GATT — and as money flowed in nanoseconds in and out of currencies and countries — such government-owned firms, which were shamelessly coddled, awarded special privileges, and run by incompetent politicians or civil servants, began to lose too much money. By 1990, privatizations in 70 capitalist and former communist countries represented the sale of $222 billion in assets.

Public enterprises have had to adapt or be absorbed. Unfortunately, Canada has not moved sufficiently quickly on this front, which poses a special problem. Not only is the debt of public enterprises a nagging burden for taxpayers, but these enterprises as constituted are inefficient and — worst of all — indifferent toward exporting. Back in 1986, roughly one-quarter of the biggest enterprises in Canada were government owned, notably the hydro utilities, and they have totally missed the boat compared with their private-sector counterparts when it comes to capitalizing on infrastructure developments abroad. Everything saleable should be sold to reduce debts. Not only would doing so reduce the cost to taxpayers, but hydro utilities and others would be forced to use their monopoly position at home as a springboard for exports or investments abroad. Now they are flabby and inefficient because they are entitled to unchallenged monopolies and need not improve their return on capital. Canada's proliferation of non–trade oriented public enterprise has hurt the country in several ways: most ignore export opportunities; most are a drain on the public purse; and many have caused trading-partner resentment, if not political trade disputes, because they are subsidized.

NEW INDUSTRIAL STRATEGIES

Canada's priority must be to slice debts in order to lower taxes as quickly as possible. This would reduce living costs, prices, and eventually wages, making the country more competitive in terms of trade and more attractive to foreign investors. But matching U.S. tax rates should not be the goal. Canada should aim to become the Switzerland or United Kingdom of the Western hemisphere and impose taxes lower than those in the United States. Such a strategy would be enlightened and beneficial, and would reverse the flow of industries, and brains, southward.

This goal is eminently achievable through drastic pruning and privatization. This decade, Americans will pay increasingly higher taxes if they are to tackle their debt and deficit problem, deal with urban blight, repair decaying infrastructure, provide universal health care to all citizens, and deal with the country's enormous social inequities. The United States faces other costs as well: it will not slash the size of its armed forces overnight and will continue to support the world's biggest, most expensive military machine. Canada has none of these burdens to support and should be able to "undercut" U.S. taxes.

Another priority should be tourism, an industry of enormous benefit to any country because it earns foreign currency and also provides the most immediate trickle-down benefits for the young and relatively unskilled. Some $26 billion in 1993 will have been spent by tourists and business visitors in Canada, ranking this industry as Canada's fourth largest. But the potential is much greater.

Travel is poorly marketed in Canada, with those and publicity efforts scattered in dozens of directions. Provinces, the federal governments, cities, industries — all wage their own advertising campaigns, some quite ineffective, when a concerted effort should be organized to target and blitz the Americans, Europeans, and Asians. Britain performs this task as well as any country does through its centralized, federal tourist board. This body is in partnership with private-sector stakeholders, such as hotels and airlines, offering package deals through selected "gateway" cities like London. There are historical tours, theatre packages, country packages. There is talk of this in Canada, but each province has its own tiny tourist empire and jealously guards its existence. Organization along centralized lines is therefore difficult, which is unfortunate because Canada is one of the world's most beautiful countries and its cities are among the most civilized and interesting. This country could, and should, be one of the world's most popular vacation destinations.

Besides scenery, Canada is blessed with agricultural riches, as are the United States and Latin America. While hard to imagine now, as farmers and fishermen leave the land and sea for economic reasons, agriculture and fishery in the next century will become one of the country's most important industries. The increasing wealth of overpopulated and over-crowded Asia will mean that the United States, Canada, Australia, and New Zealand will become the world's bread-baskets, with their large land masses, climates, technologies, and efficient practitioners.

Unfortunately, these four countries have been battling Europe and Japan to scrap some of the subsidies that drive down prices as cheap European produce, meat, and other foodstuffs are dumped onto world markets. The Japanese don't subsidize exports, but do subsidize domestic farmers, and impose quotas on certain commodities, such as rice. Eventually, compromises will be reached or the latest GATT discussions won't proceed. That would hurt everyone.

Of course, totally free, non-tariff trade in agriculture is impossible because food is too important to be left to the free market. Agricultural policy is part social, military, and environmental policy, as well as economic policy. Countries want to retain their own security of food supplies in case of war or trade disruption. Countries need farmers to look after the land, a precious national resource. And nations must support farmers because the market is rigged heavily through massive government subsidies, costing Americans and Europeans as much as US$60 billion a year.

To stay in the game, Canada has rightly supported its farmers, but the cost of doing so for a relatively small country such as ours is enormous. The Tories in Ottawa have spent as much as $20 million in eight years, propping up the country's wheat farmers alone, as Americans and Europeans subsidized wheat down to rock-bottom prices.

But Canada's system of subsidies for milk, eggs, chickens, and turkeys should be scrapped. Called supply management, quotas are set for these commodities in order to prop up prices. Consumers end up paying through the nose as prices are based on guaranteeing profits to the least efficient, or most indebted, producers. The result is these commodities are as much as 50 per cent more expensive here than south of the border and — along with cigarettes and alcohol — are the principal reason behind excessive cross-border shopping by Canadians.

No country has a free-market system in agriculture, but Canada's policy makers should adopt for these commodities the type of income supports, rather than consumer supports, that exist in the United States. Otherwise, they will continue to lose tax revenues and economic activity as Canadians avoid taxes by shopping in U.S. supermarkets.

The world will never have a free market in agriculture, said Dwayne Andreas, chairman and CEO of agri-food conglomerate Archer, Daniels, Midland Company of Decatur, Illinois, in an interview in 1993. Even if a free market was achievable, it would create a dangerous environmental problem because farmers would compete wildly, taking shortcuts and depleting the world's already diminishing topsoil. "And we have used up half the topsoil in the world already. In 50 years, the U.S. will have huge problems and in 100 years it will be a crisis," he said.

Because of the importance of Canada's agricultural resources, governments must continue to invest in biotech research into soil-protection technologies, hydroponics, and other agricultural innovations. Canada should also aim to add value to our agricultural output wherever possible. For instance, Alberta beef producers have begun to ship tailor-made cut meats — not sides of beef — to Japan, according to customer specifications. The Japanese pay exorbitant amounts for food because their domestic sector is so inefficient and expensive. Similarly, seafood from Canada's East and West coasts enjoy tremendous success in Japan, despite transportation costs, and one Vancouver company has been shipping tonnes of ice cream made in Canada.

Andreas has invested $400 million in Canadian agriculture industries since free trade with the United States, and will invest more building processing plants to mill flour or make soybean protein and other products if freight-rate subsidies to seaports for exports are ended, he said. "More value can be added to farm products. If freight rates are equal to, or more than, the cost of processing, then the processing will be done at source. Canada and the United States share a colonial mentality, but you have been slower at getting rid of it. Now it's cheaper for a Japanese processor to process in Japan than here in Canada."

Canadians also have other assets they don't adequately market, such as tolerance, safety, and space. The Japanese government, for instance, looked at two innovative schemes recently, and Canada should resurrect both. One in Australia was called "Silver City" and involved building a complete retirement community for 25,000 Japanese people. These retirees were to be given special status to live in Australia, and interest would have been significant. Japanese living and housing costs are exorbitant compared with Australia's. But local resistance scrapped the scheme, even though the community would have brought billions of dollars of economic activity to the country through construction and services to retirees. Canada should seek to create such communities in order to attract their billions of dollars of economic activity.

Another proposal involved moving an entire city of 50,000 people to rural Montana. Some 10 Japanese multinationals would establish North American headquarters with thousands of employees in this free-enterprise zone. But, once more, local resistance was great, and the 10 firms decided against locating far from financial capitals. Canada should also try to attract the head office of every transnational corporation in the world that is not already established in North America.

While selective immigration should be allowed as part of an industrial strategy, Canada should scrap its current immigration policy altogether. Until unemployment levels fall below 5 or 6 per cent, only well-heeled wealth creators who will invest or start businesses should be allowed in. Right now, Canada's fast-track citizenship requires an investment of $350,000 or the employment of several Canadians. But any others allowed into our economy should be given temporary work permits only, not full-fledged immigration status. And preference should be given to Americans and Mexicans. This would serve several purposes. Canada could export those migrants who become unemployed, thus reducing its unemployment burden. But by giving preference to American and Mexican migrants, Canada would be helping to ease their unemployment problems at the same time. The United States would probably return the favour, thus allowing Canadians to move to where the work is if taxes here drive companies to the states.

Canada should also put together a swat team of business

experts to conduct an inventory of transnationals that are not in Canada to determine how they could be enticed here. Then whatever it takes should be done. For instance, Liberal Paul Martin Jr. told a story of how Canada could get 400 research jobs from Germany. "I asked the head of a large German multinational faced with the excessive costs of doing business back home what it would take to get his company's research division with 400 scientists," recalled Martin. "He told me that if a Canadian university created three chairs of environmental engineering and attracted three of the best academics in this field, they would move immediately."

Similarly, Harvard University recently wooed a Canadian to its academic ranks as visiting professor but overcame one of the man's objections by allowing his children to attend the university as visiting students. In other cases, immigration policies were bent to allow entry to highly desirable persons. Such aggressiveness is going to be more and more necessary as foreign investors are courted by countries all over the world. Canada no longer can count on investors finding, and developing, our economy. We must market the country.

To do this, External Affairs must be gutted and revamped. One of the striking characteristics of Canada's embassies and consulates abroad is the fact that most of External's officers who handle trade matters have never met a payroll, and few, if any, hold commerce, economics, or finance degrees of any description. Virtually all trade officers are career diplomats who majored in foreign languages and liberal arts. Most lack moxie or street smarts, and some have outright contempt for businessmen. They would rather be political officers than trade officers.

Other countries do much better at the task of enhancing

trade abroad. Germany's consulates work closely with its chambers of commerce, thus marrying diplomatic connections with business networks. Better yet, Canada should employ, on contract in its trade missions abroad, private-sector experts who can feed industrial and financial intelligence back to the business community.

We should also develop a "trade corps" — a program by which young business graduates from colleges as well as universities could work at embassies abroad. Their task would be to gather industrial intelligence, learn a foreign language, and establish business links to market back home. The hope would be that these young people could facilitate trade deals in the countries in which they served. Similarly, External Affairs should welcome more trade representatives in its offices, drawn from, and paid for by, sectors or industry organizations. Executives, sales personnel, and analysts would welcome the opportunity to be seconded for two or three years to foreign countries, again with a view toward developing contacts down the road.

In addition, Canada must develop an élite corps of business managers. Canadians have the world's best hockey players because we have developed one of the world's best hockey training systems. But Canadians do not have the world's best baseball players or business managers. The Americans do, because they have the best baseball, and business, training systems in the world. One of the ways to create top-notch schools of management is to let the universities privatize their business schools. These institutions would become highly profitable because corporations and individuals would pay handsomely, thus allowing them to hire the best instructors and experts in the world for students.

Another important "trade" policy is Canada's continued

support for the many international institutions it belongs to, from GATT to the Commonwealth, Organization of American States, NATO, the United Nations, Pacific Rim associations, and so on. In fact, few countries have as many networks as Canada has that can become an important conduit for conducting business abroad. Unfortunately, these memberships also result in expensive responsibilities. And as the United States slowly withdraws from its role as the world's policeman, Canada and the others must take up the slack. The United Nations' peacekeeping burdens that Canada has accepted must, and will, continue as a *de facto* world government forms with its own multinational police force. Those burdens, plus the need to eliminate deficits and lower taxes, cannot be shouldered without some serious surgery to Canada's spending. This requirement will dominate Canadian politics in the 1990s and determine whether the country's living standards will decline or rise.

THE BRITISH DISEASE

Canada was not called British North America without reason. Its economy, particularly after the Second World War, has aped the Mother Country's unaffordable cradle-to-grave system. Now like Britain, Canada needs a strong leader like Margaret Thatcher to unravel the mess and streamline government, privatize everything, impose democracy on the undemocratic union movement, and, ideally, convert the country into a tax haven.

But the restructuring of governments, as well as of our health, education, and welfare systems, must be almost as sweeping as what the Czechs and Poles have undertaken.

Too many Canadians are already living off the state, unconcerned with competition or competitiveness. About half the workforce is either not profit-oriented or is living totally off the other half in the form of state subsidies. In Ontario — the wealthiest province, with 40 per cent of the national GDP — one out of every four able-bodied adults works for a government, and another one out of every four collects welfare, unemployment insurance, or some other entitlement. Meanwhile, an estimated 600,000 jobs went begging in mid-1993, and the underground economy thrived. Farmers, restaurateurs, renovators, and other small enterprises routinely complained because they could not entice people to leave their entitlements unless they paid them cash under the table. Meanwhile, those same businessmen were having to pay higher taxes because black-market workers were collecting entitlements.

By 1993, with deficits climbing, it became apparent that Canada was afflicted with the British disease. Never before has so much been paid to so many by so few. The Maritimes was a third-world economy. Quebec sank slowly, unable to plug into the global economy without subsidy because of its language barrier. Even prosperous Ontario rang up a deficit of $9 billion, higher than the deficits posted by the vast majority of countries.

Unlike the republic to the south preoccupied with the Cold War, Canada after the Second World War quickly embraced Britain's notion of the welfare state. Now, like most European countries, Canada offers an array of entitlements that are so open ended and generous that they form a major disincentive to work among low-wage earners. The result is a chronic unemployment problem self-created by entitlements. At current rates, a welfare recipient in Toronto with three dependents cannot afford to work unless he or she can make about $35,000 a year, or $20 an hour. Conversely, breadwinners making less than $20 an hour cannot afford to work. This handcuffs low-wage earners to entitlements forever.

By comparison, in Sweden, welfare payments are granted for 18 months to persons under 57 years of age, and only slightly longer for those older. While receiving financial help, Swedes must perform public service without pay unless they are taking retraining. Because there is a deadline on help, Swedes seek training or hunt aggressively for work. If the deadline passes, they are forced to accept whatever job they can find, or live off relatives and friends. This policy is enlightened for two reasons. Its structure encourages work search, public service, or training, and has also helped Sweden maintain the lowest wage-inflation levels in Europe. In Canada or Britain, by contrast, the $20-an-hour welfare entitlement for a person with three dependents becomes a *de facto* minimum wage, which forces all wages up unnecessarily.

Canada's health system has been another problem. In 1975, health-care costs totalled C$12.267 billion for 22.697 million Canadians, or 7.2 per cent of GNP and $540 per head. By 1990, this figure had grown to $61.753 billion for 26.6 million or 9.2 per cent of GNP and $2,321 per head. The problem with Canada's system is that there is no discipline. Patients can overdemand, and doctors can overservice. People can routinely demand third, fourth, and fifth opinions on medical procedures, cosmetic surgery, or even hair removal. Doctors can order too many tests or too many repeat visits without complaint because extra services do not cost patients a dime. Fraud is potentially rampant too, because patients don't even see a copy of the invoice sent to the government by their physicians.

Besides fees, medical overheads are enormous. In the good years, politicians have littered the landscape with political hospitals, political clinics, political medical equipment. Now with financial constraints everywhere, the downsizing has been about as nonsensical as the expansion phase was. Instead of closing down hospitals and rationalizing the system through specialization, officials routinely close beds in all hospitals. This guarantees that all hospitals will become even more of a drain on taxpayers because fewer beds mean underutilization.

The answer is for the federal government to allow user fees. In addition, medical care should become a taxable benefit of up to 5 per cent of annual income added to an individual's income for tax purposes. User fees will introduce discipline to a system which is now like a smorgasbord. Consumers can have anything they want in whatever quantity they wish and end up digesting too much. Overuse without consequences, and the potential for fraud among doctors, are responsible for soaring, unsustainable medical costs in Canada.

Health-care reform is a priority because the Canadian population is rapidly aging, and medical costs rise tenfold after age 65. The changing demographics of the country also mean that government pension benefits should not kick in until age 65, instead of at 60, as is now the option. People are living longer, and the savings would be gigantic. Another important pension reform involves the trimming of excessively generous pensions for public-sector workers. These are indexed and should not be. And frills such as the arrangement by which paid sick days can be saved over years, then used to move up the date of retirement, should be scrapped immediately.

Like health, education is one of the most important jobs any society performs, and Canada has certainly flunked the test in some respects. Teacher credentials are high, facilities are first class, and the country spends as much as the United States or any other country in the world on education. But something is very wrong when high school drop-out rates are 30 per cent, illiteracy is estimated at 25 per cent, and innumeracy is probably even more prevalent.

The educational establishment must take the lion's share of the blame. Teachers' unions in the past have seemed more preoccupied with reducing class sizes and increasing salaries than with the quality of the "product" being churned out. Regimentation and discipline have disappeared and been replaced with child-centred learning that is an abysmal failure for either backward or behaviourally difficult pupils. Most children need to be sped along at a regimented pace along with their peers, not left to individual studies or their own devices. Educators in Anglo-Saxon countries have been more concerned about feel-good education — or social engineering — than with getting on with teaching the basics. Students need to learn how to read, not to learn how to tolerate homosexuality. They need more math, not more curriculum options. They need computer skills, not sex education. Above all, the disinclination to "subject" children to competitions such as spelling bees, grades, or streaming is a hypocritical denial of the world into which they will graduate. Schools must encourage competition, not avoid it.

Canada should neither cut, nor increase, education expenditures. We spend as much as any country, but we should spend it more wisely. At last, there are signs that the public has begun to resist the routine property-tax hikes that have accompanied the constant caving in to teachers' unions over the years. This is where most of the money has gone.

But what the public wants, and deserves, is better results. As rationalization must take place in health care, so educators must specialize and hive off excess facilities to save money. Schools in areas of declining enrolment must be forced to close once certain thresholds are reached. Some school boards maintain this policy is already in place, but there are plenty of examples of children attending half-empty schools with two or three grades taught in one classroom just so that kids can walk to school and the principal can save his or her job.

While Canada's educational system is a lot better than the U.S. system, which discriminates against the poor, it is no reason for us to be smug. Virtually all of our other major trading partners — in Europe and Asia — do a significantly better job of educating than we do. Their children attend school 11 months per year in most cases, and so should ours. They also impose more discipline on their youngsters through the use of uniforms and regimentation, which force pupils at all levels to move quickly through considerably more material. Our schools should do the same. Finally, standardized testing should be imposed, in order to grade the performance of teachers.

Critics say that more stringent systems of education stifle individualism and creativity. They also, quite rightly, point out that European and Asian societies lack the inventiveness that characterizes Britain, Canada, and the United States. For instance, more Nobel prizes have been won by alumni from Oxford University than by the whole of Japan.

But these prizes were not won by high school drop-outs or semi-literates who graduate with the bare essentials. Besides, the Japanese are catching up in terms of patents and Nobels. Irrefutably, the most stunning difference between Asia's successful economies and ours is that education is valued more highly than any other endeavour.

Canada's post-secondary system of education should be restructured, and students should pay considerably higher user-fees. Higher costs will force students to work harder and to pick occupationally oriented courses. More expense will also encourage parents to supervise their children more closely to ensure that they are not wasting their time in universities or colleges, or our money. The annual subsidy for an undergraduate in Ontario is nearly $10,000. Like our health system, the heavily subsidized education system is victim to both overdemand and overservicing. Professors and university administrators are disinclined to discourage students because their budgets are based on enrolment figures.

Another British disease in Canada has been the epidemic of the "council" or public-housing phenomenon. Ontario is now North America's largest landlord, with some 100,000 publicly assisted housing units, often occupied by persons who don't need the subsidy. As well, a raft of other housing programs — federal, provincial, and municipal — across the country syphon off billions of dollars of annual taxpayer subsidies and give them to people who often do not require the help. The rationale for this system has been that politicians do not wish to stigmatize the poor and clump them into highrise buildings. Now they build low-rise public housing and fill it with tenants who are poor and those who need no rent subsidy. Unfortunately, the market-value rents never match the cost of building the units — typically $152,000 in

1993 for a two-bedroom unit — thus conferring a $1,000 a month or more benefit to the tenant.

Governments must get out of the housing business altogether for several reasons. Civil servants have no idea how to tender or build economically viable units, so the result is overbuilding, expensive building, and needless building. Those who need rent subsidies should be given them and allowed to live wherever they wish. Thus, stigmatization would be avoided and the public would be spared the expense of building units for people who can afford to live anywhere. As for those already in public housing, governments should issue each tenant a taxable-benefits slip in the amount of his or her entitlement.

Public housing should be totally privatized. Margaret Thatcher, for instance, sold virtually all of Britain's council houses in the 1980s to get the government out from under the expense of being a landlord. All of these decisions are tough, if not impossible, for elected politicians to make.

That is why Canada must adopt two policy reforms: free votes for elected representatives in the House of Commons so they can be sensitive to their constituents' wishes and not those of cabinet, and routine referendums on major social and economic issues. These reforms would mean that the people who foot the bill will be consulted all the time — not just the noisy, politically involved people who are paid to represent groups, lobbies, corporations, unions, or causes.

Referendums may be the only means of tackling effectively the debt and deficit problem, as they allow politicians to pass the buck. Voters should be forced to make the choices: cut or tax. A referendum question, for instance, could ask voters if they want any tax increases for the next five years or not. And which items on a list of alternatives complete, with estimated cost savings, should be cut. A debate leading up to the vote would ensue, and consequences would be discussed. Without such referendums, the politicians — no matter how strong — will never be able to tackle the tough stuff head on. Instead, they will have to be machiavellian and equivocal, speaking out of both sides of their mouths and talking deficit reduction without specifics.

Unfortunately, such behaviour has created cynicism. Most voters are disenchanted and have become inclined to punish, rather than vote, for politicians. The election of a socialist regime in Ontario is a case in point. There is no way that 37 per cent of the population would have voted for a government that would ratchet up health, education, and welfare costs by 34 per cent and run up a deficit the size of most sovereign nations. The election of socialists in Ontario, as in Saskatchewan or B.C., was strictly a protest vote against the two mainstream parties. Voter cynicism means that no politician can win the trust of the electorate; therefore, the country must be governed by a structure of guaranteed voter participation through referendums.

TAKING ON CANADA'S UNIONS

Margaret Thatcher stared down the unions, and so must Canada. Inordinately high levels of unionization have made our living costs jump and reduced wage flexibility, thus driving jobs out of the country. That situation has also hurt Germany's economy and has driven jobs offshore for the first time in the country's postwar history. Germany's much-vaunted partnership between government, unions, and business is in total disrepute since the fall of the Iron Curtain and increasing competition in the global economy. The problem plaguing Germany is identical to Canada's: if unions are unwilling to let their workers accept, or even vote upon, wage or other concessions, companies have no choice but to replace them with machines, if possible, or to move to a jurisdiction with cheaper labour rates. The lack of wage flexibility in a competitive environment seriously hobbles corporations and countries.

About 35 per cent of Canada's workforce is unionized (18 per cent of the private sector, and nearly 100 per cent in the public sector). The problem is not so much with private-sector unions, which are slightly more responsive to the economic reality, but public sector unions. During the recession in the early 1990s, for instance, the country's taxpayers, mostly non-unionized workers, were forced to accept less, as were their companies. And yet both individuals and companies were forced, through their taxes, to support unionized workers in government or public enterprises, and monopolies who refuse to accept similar pay or fringe-benefit declines.

Canada's weak politicians routinely cave in because union leaders are incredibly powerful, collecting some C$800 million in dues in 1988, or — as in the case of the New Democrats — because opposing the unions represents a conflict of interest because their principal supporters are public-sector union leaders. These leaders also function like dictators and use their funds to finance special-interest groups to further causes and socialism. There are rarely secret-ballot referendums within unions asking union members whether they agree or not. Even worse, when union rank and file try to exercise their democratic rights by challenging union affiliations, leaders use dues collected from captive members to fight against their own workers.

"The Canadian Auto Workers union used our money to fight us in the [May 1993] referenda to kick out the New Democratic Party affiliation," said Doug Gammie, an auto worker in Oshawa, Ontario. He and others successfully waged a campaign in 1993 to disaffiliate their local — the auto workers' largest in Canada, with 24,000 members — from the NDP because the party did not represent members' views. They circulated a petition demanding a referendum, held the vote, and won overwhelmingly to disaffiliate. "But there were smear campaigns and they used our money to fight us. That's not democratic," said Gammie.

Unfortunately, such battles require dedication, money, and tenacity. Canada is a closed shop, thanks to the notorious Rand Formula that forces workers to pay dues if they join a union shop. But the Rand Formula can be struck down: individuals have the right to assemble in order to collectively bargain, but the converse is not true. As it stands, individuals in Canada are forced to support financially unions they don't want to join.

British Columbia's laws actually go beyond the Rand Formula and clearly transgress civil rights by forcing workers to join a union against their will. A test case was launched in 1993, with the help of the National Citizens Coalition, to help Norma Janzen, age 52, a teacher of learning-disabled children who was fired in 1990 because she refused to join a union.

For 24 years, Janzen taught children with special needs when, in June 1990, her school board and union negotiated a closed-shop provision. She refused to join both the union and the British Columbia Teachers Federation and was deprived of her means of making a living as a result.

"I entered this profession because I wanted to help young people, and joining the union would have interfered with that goal," she said. "I had to stand by that principle even if it meant losing my job. Someone has to stand up for what's right. These laws which infringe on my freedom of association are just plain wrong."

The coalition will pay her costs, and was contacted by a group called BC Teachers for Association, acting on her behalf. In Janzen's district of Langley, teachers were given one year to join the union. Those opposed appealed their case to the Industrial Relations Council, but were unsuccessful. Janzen's lawyer will argue that closed shops violate an individual's freedom of association, guaranteed by section 2(d) of the Canadian Charter of Rights and Freedoms. She will also seek damages from the school board.

Another problem is that provincial labour laws make decertification extraordinarily difficult. Companies are often forced to shut down and move to the United States in order to get out from under a union. These restrictions can become silly if applied faithfully. An Ontario electrician who had to lay off all his employees in 1992 was forbidden, as an individual, from working without a union card because his workers had not voted in favour of decertification. The problem was he had no workers to vote on whether to decertify or not. It was a Catch-22, and he has been denied the right to work by the union and province.

Even worse is the situation in Quebec where construction unions have made powerful political friends. There laws forbid construction workers without union cards to work unless they obtain a permit from the Quebec Construction Commission. These are stingily meted out, and workers routinely work "illegally," as do contractors who hire them.

Gâtineau, Québec, contractor Jocelyn Dumais has led a one-man campaign against such practices after being prosecuted for the crime of working. "Usually about half the guys on a construction site are working without a permit, and the commission inspectors suddenly arrive and everybody runs like hell to get away," he said. "It's not right that Quebeckers are denied the right to work in their own province at the wages they want to work for. Workers are fined hundreds per occurrence, and employers thousands, and I know guys who have gone to jail for this."

Unbelievable, but true. Even worse, Quebec's restrictive labour law drives Quebec workers to neighbouring provinces where there are no restrictions. At the same time, Quebec forbids out-of-province workers or contractors to operate inside its borders. As a result, in 1993 New Brunswick and the City of Ottawa banned Quebec workers from their regions until Quebec lifts restrictions against construction workers or contractors from out of the province.

Such laws undermine civil rights. But they are also very bad economics because they prohibit Canadians and their union-shop employers from having the type of wage flexibility they need to match rivals' prices in hard times or competitive markets. In any country around the world, the existence of intractable and unreasonable unions guarantees the export of jobs as well as automation. As for public-sector unions, they must be prohibited from striking and be forced to accept pay cuts when the economy is not performing as well as it has been.

Reforms must also be undertaken as to the way public-sector employees are paid. Currently, they are paid according to position and seniority. They should receive merit pay too. Under the current system, the best teachers or civil servants don't make enough, and the inefficient ones make too much. Merit pay would reward productive workers and provide an incentive for the less efficient to work harder. In addition, public-sector workers should be harnessed to help cut the deficit through a system of awards and bonuses to those who come up with cost-cutting measures.

CONCLUSION

One of the more interesting benefits of the new world restructuring is that Canada's perennial, and tiresome, separatism debate will become irrelevant in the 1990s. Within one generation, Quebec's 4.5-million French Canadians will likely be part of a hemispheric trading bloc comprising 330 million anglophones, 400 million Latin Americans, and only a few million desperately poor francophones in Haiti. That means that, whether Quebec remains a province or becomes a separate country, Quebeckers must survive in an ocean of anglophones and, with French unilingualism no longer an option, the most important reason cited by separatists for Quebec's leaving Canada no longer exists.

In the next century, Canada, as well as any independent regime in Quebec, will become more and more economically dependent upon the rest of North America. At the same time, as the United States continues to retreat from its traditional role as the world's policeman and benefactor and the United Nations takes on those tasks instead, Canada will have a greater say and more influence over world events than it has ever enjoyed.

We have had a preview of what this shift will mean. In the early 1990s, Canada's tiny armed forces were deployed in U.N. actions around the world and stretched to the limit providing troops in former Yugoslavia, Somalia, and Cambodia. This financial burden will increase in future, and be shared by the largest and richest countries, including Canada, Germany, Britain, France, Italy, and Japan. Likewise, these nations will be expected to pull more of their weight when it comes to providing financial aid to the world's outcasts or in the event of natural disasters. Already a global government has formed through the auspices of the United Nations and the G-7 process.

This development is welcome and badly needed, particularly because the world's overriding problem — overpopulation — can be attacked only through a global effort. Unfortunately, the greatest failure of the U.N. Rio de Janeiro "Earth Summit" was that the issue of overpopulation was stricken from its agenda in response to pressure from the Vatican. The world must mount a war against high fertility rates by making available birth control and education. China, with its one-child-per-couple Family Planning Act, has shown what can be done in just one generation. Estimates are that China's act single-handedly prevented the birth of 240 million. Brazil, through less Draconian means, has also dramatically reduced birth rates from 4.7 children per female in 1975 to 3.5 per female by 1986.

Besides an all-out campaign to limit population, new technologies must be devised to reverse ecological damage and replace destructive behaviour such as hydrocarbon burning and pollution of water and air. As well as governments, large transnational corporations with huge research budgets must be harnessed. The 10 largest transnationals in the United States spent more on research and development annually than France and Britain combined. Besides searching for solutions, rich countries will have to subsidize poor ones so they may clean up their air, water, and industries.

Most important, the world's richest nations must accelerate the process of redistribution of wealth through trade and aid policies. Poor nations, in return, must be encouraged to adopt the enlightened socioeconomic and environmental policies of rich countries. Redistribution has been well advanced already within industrialized countries. But there has been resistance to aid or free trade in wealthy countries. Unfortunately, if protectionists and isolationists get their way, the world in the twenty-first century will be mean, plagued with starvation, terrorism, and environmental catastrophe.

Free trade is mutually beneficial. Once-poor countries like Taiwan provided rich countries with cheap imported goods until they became rich themselves. Now Taiwan is busy investing in poor neighbours, such as Thailand and mainland China, as well as in the improvement of its own quality of life through the building of subways, sewage systems, and improved housing. Taiwan, after 40 years of hard work, now doles out foreign aid to Russia and others.

Free trade has also solved the overpopulation problem wherever it has resulted in higher living standards. Birth rates fall precipitously in societies where women are educated and can ensure their family's future by working.

Besides those benefits, trade opportunities can be used to bring about enlightened policies and cleaner economic growth. By offering preferential market access and special tariff arrangements, the United States was able to get Mexico to begin to clean up its environmental act. Washington's threat to suspend its "most-favoured nation" tariff benefits to China led to its release of hundreds of dissident students jailed after Tiananmen Square. Likewise, Japan's generous aid to China has been strictly earmarked for use in cleaning up the environment there.

Feeding the world's hungry is another priority. Agriculture tycoon Dwayne Andreas told the United Nations in June 1993: "Forget about having a U.N. army. What we need now, and fast, is to get involved in world food problems. Why weren't hungry people at GATT? Why weren't the Africans there? Instead, we had cartels there deciding how to cut production to keep prices up."

The world's agriculture should be organized along the lines of the Canadian Wheat Board, which estimates crop supplies, pays before harvest, finds export markets, and distributes food to needy countries. The world must feed the hungry, and can if a system of distribution is created, subsidized by rich countries.

In these and other areas, Canada will play an increasingly important role in determining the future direction of this planet. But only if we get our own house in order. Canadians this decade are at a crossroads and don't realize it. The world has changed beyond our borders, our leaders have thoroughly mismanaged our affairs, and some tough choices await us before the century turns. While the prospect is unpleasant, we cannot indulge in self-pity. Our problems were not imposed on us by others, but self-created by a political élite that has been short-sighted and reckless. While cutting back and reducing the role of governments may be tough, Canadians should thank their lucky stars that they do not have the problems faced by Africans or Ukrainians or Chinese or Iranians. The world is much safer now that the threat of nuclear Armageddon and the superpower arms race is finished. That safety allows us to concentrate on making a better world. And Canadians need only learn how to live within their means and improve upon what already is done well here. This task is not a matter for academic debate. Nor is it a platform issue for left and right or Tories and socialists. It is a matter of survival.